What a "Friend" We Had in Bill

William F. Buckley, Jr.
and the Rise, Betrayal, and
Fall of Starr Broadcasting

Michael F. Starr

Stroud & Hall Publishers
www.stroudhall.com

Library of Congress Cataloging-in-Publication Data

Starr, Michael F., 1940-
What a "friend" we had in Bill : William F. Buckley and the rise, betrayal, and fall of Starr
Broadcasting / By Michael F. Starr.
 pages cm
Includes bibliographical references and index.
ISBN 978-0-9893373-5-9 (pbk. : alk. paper)
1. Starr, Michael F., 1940- 2. Starr, Peter H., 1941-1991. 3. Buckley, William F., Jr., 1925-2008--
Influence. 4. Starr Broadcasting Group. 5. Mass media--United States--Biography. 6.
Businessmen--United States--Biography. I. Title.
P92.5.A1A3 2015
384.545'2092--dc23
[B]
                        2015022639

Disclaimer of Liability: With respect to statements of opinion or fact available in this work of nonfiction, Stroud & Hall Publishers nor any of its employees makes any warranty, express or implied, or assumes any legal liability or responsibility for the accuracy or completeness of any information disclosed, or represents that its use would not infringe privately-owned rights.

For Peter H. Starr—We miss you so...

This book is about the long-term relationship between conservative writer and broadcaster William F. "Bill" Buckley, Jr. and the Starr brothers: Michael and Peter. It tells the story of the broadcasting company the Starrs built together in the mid-1960s and its collapse in the mid-1970s. What began as a warm mentor-protégé relationship fell apart under the cloud of an investigation by the Securities and Exchange Commission and ended in mistrust, acrimony, and the early death of Peter, who had the strongest ties with Bill Buckley.

The author, Michael "Mike" Starr, dedicates the book to his late brother. In these pages, Mike chronicles the events of his own life and those of the company, how two young men took Bill Buckley's little Omaha, Nebraska radio station and built it into a major radio and TV operation. Highly respected in an industry that would later be taken over by super-sized corporations with little regard for hometowns and hard work, Starr Broadcasting Group served as a grassroots boon for more than ten years. Bill Buckley was the "prestige" of the Starr Broadcasting Group, but Peter and Mike were the "heartbeat."

Table of Contents

Introduction

The *Orlando Sentinel* said it this way:

> Peter H. Starr, 49, president of Southern Starr Broadcasting Group
> Inc. of Winter Park, died early Sunday (July 21). Southern Starr
> Broadcasting is a publicly held Winter Park company that owns
> and operates radio stations. Starr began his broadcasting career in
> 1964 in Omaha, Neb., at an AM-FM station after graduating from
> Georgetown University in Washington. Two years later, Starr
> founded Starr Broadcasting Group Inc., which at one point owned
> 14 radio stations and TV properties from New York to Honolulu.
> After selling Starr Broadcasting to Shamrock Communications Inc.,
> Starr founded Southern Starr Broadcasting in 1983.[1]

It had been a difficult number of years since my brother Peter and
I were shot at sunrise at Starr Broadcasting. I first realized that I
wanted to do something to right what I considered to be the wrong
of Peter's untimely death—and of our joint careers—in 1991 when I
was standing in the graveyard where Peter was being buried. His wife
Sandy, with whom I did not get along, was talking with the people
who had been involved with Starr Broadcasting and Southern Starr
Broadcasting, and nobody was speaking to me. I said to myself, *they
want what Sandy's got now, and what I want is for people to know the
real story.*

I remember that Bill Buckley did not show up for the funeral.
Couldn't make it. I think he sent some flowers.

I talked to Bill Buckley a couple of times after that, including a dinner party in 1989 at Southern Illinois University where he was the main speaker honoring the president of SIU. Before the dinner we spoke for about twenty minutes and he told me that it had been the most difficult time of his life—the whole Starr saga—and he said he lost his control, that he didn't know what he was doing. He wanted to talk about what Peter's situation was and I told him that Peter and I had started the new Southern Starr company. I explained that it was doing really well, but Peter's personal life was a mess.

I had seen a card Bill wrote in 1985, after the demise of Starr Broadcasting, saying "Dear Peter, Delighted to learn all is going so well with you, commercially, biologically and otherwise. Warm regards, Bill." Bill had received bad information, and I hoped our conversation in 1989 corrected that, but I'm not sure.

In 1991 I had just come back from a cruise with Peter and I knew it would be the last time I would ever see him alive. I told that to my wife, Ruth. She was ready to head home and tried to coax me, saying "Let's go get in the car." I told her, "I don't want to. I don't think I'm ever going to see him again." And I was right.

It seemed like such a daunting task to sit down and write Peter's and my side that for years and years I maintained what I called The Buckley Box, collecting any information I found that I thought would be useful: articles, photos, old documents when I could find them (I got out of the company with very few records). I didn't know where I was going to even start such a project as this, but I began at least to write an outline. After finishing and looking it back over, I finally thought, *Maybe I can do this.* Slowly, I began to put together the story that I first determined to tell back in that cemetery in 1991.

Cast of Characters

Throughout this book you will see quotes from some of the people who have been instrumental in not only the creation and growth of Starr Broadcasting, but in the telling of the Starr story itself. Each contributor will be helping to move the story along by revealing their own experiences and feelings throughout the story. After all, some of them were privy to things Peter and I weren't at the time, and they each had their own interactions with and opinions of Bill Buckley.

When you see the name of one of these people before a block-quote, it means he or she is telling how he was involved or her view of a certain event. He might even be revealing information that I did not know before I conducted the exclusive interviews for this project.

As you continue to read, you will find out more and more about these people, but I want to briefly introduce each of them here.

Jim Long is president of Telos Holdings in Malibu, California. His original involvement with Starr was as co-founder of TM Productions, the group that made our radio stations sound as great on the air as they did. Jim's company used jingles, produced commercials, and conducted "image" building, which involved developing a particular "sound" for each Starr radio station's format. TM was recognized as the best in the business.

Jim also played a big part in the unmasking of Bill Buckley during the Securities and Exchange Commission investigation of Starr Broadcasting in 1976.

Ed McConwell, as you will discover, became my friend during the early period of Starr's acquisitions. Without "spoiling" a pretty good tale, I will simply tell you that Ed, in his capacity as an attorney for his father-in-law during our purchase of his Kansas City radio station, saved my bacon. I made a huge financial mistake that Ed could have taken advantage of, but did not. Peter and I got to know Ed well during that time and he has been my good friend ever since.

John Starr, one of the four Starr Brothers, will shed light on his relationship with our brother Peter. Peter captained Bill Buckley's boats and John worked with Peter on them. He will tell of the time when Peter went missing in one of Bill's vessels and of an experience he had in the middle of the racial tension sparked by a white-owned New Orleans radio station staffed exclusively by African-American talent that provided music for the black community. At one time or another, all four of the Starr boys worked for Starr Broadcasting. John was a disc jockey and a very good salesman, and went on to a longtime career in radio management in Florida, where he also teaches communications at the University of Florida.

Paul Starr, the youngest of the Starr brothers, spent a lot of time overseeing public affairs programming for Starr Broadcasting, which is why he also found himself right in the middle of a tense drama in the Bay area of Oakland-San Francisco as we tried to acquire station KABL-AM. Paul's description of Peter's confrontation with minority community leaders details one of the flash points of this book, an event which demonstrated Peter's loyalty, leadership, and mental toughness as well as his sense of fairness.

Don White was the real estate broker who put the Starr brothers in touch with a California company that owned several drive-in theaters in Texas. Don explains how the Starrs, as part of the SITCO corporation, bought the theater properties. It was this transaction that was targeted by the Securities and Exchange Commission and led to the end of our time at Starr Broadcasting and the end of our friendship with Bill Buckley.

Douglas E. Hall is not one of the "Starr Family Players," but he is the center of an incident that caused me great concern, and frankly made me mad as hell. Douglas Hall owned the Hall Radio Report, which in 1976 told of the mostly unknown (at the time) investigation of Buckley and Starr by the Securities and Exchange Commission, and received an award from Buckley for his reporting. I felt that Hall might have been "used" by Buckley, but Hall has been good enough to tell us his perspective on the situation and defend his report for this book.

Ruth Starr is my wife of three and a half decades and the "star" of the show in my life. She has been my help and support since 1980. She tells the story of how we met and how I predicted we would get together. She is aware of a great deal of the Starr Saga without ever having met Bill Buckley. She also introduced me to her son, Jim, who became my great friend and co-worker, as well as my own adopted son.

I wish to thank each of these generous friends for their contributions to this book. Peter Starr is not here to tell the story with me, but these others *were* there and *What a "Friend" We Had in Bill* would not have been possible without them.

In putting this book together I have had to rely on my memories, certainly, but those were helped along by exhaustive research. Many of the historical events I talk about—involving both Starr Broadcasting and the industry in general—are officially noted by citations and endnotes. But others, especially our acquisitions of properties and stations, if they are not specifically cited, most likely did come both from my memories and/or news reports from publications of the industry, notably *Broadcasting* and *Billboard* magazines.

Chapter 1

The Starrs Are Born

My brother Peter was born on December 6, 1941 and the next day all hell broke loose.

It wasn't his fault. It was the Japanese. They bombed Pearl Harbor and dragged us into World War II.

For some reason Peter's birthday never got lost, though it fell so close to that day which lives in infamy. The date seems particularly appropriate now, knowing how Peter and I were victims of another sneak attack, but our own "days of infamy" came in mid-summer, 1976.

My own appearance was not as dramatic as Peter's. I made my debut on October 4, 1940 at Miller Hospital in St. Paul, Minnesota. I don't remember anything about St. Paul at that time because I was basically a newborn. All I remember is that soon there was another creature called Peter. We were nigh inseparable until Peter died way too young.

My mother was Marjorie LaBrande Starr. Her family was from Louisiana, and they had a plantation on River Road north of New Orleans. After the Civil War they relocated to Indianapolis, then to St. Paul. My grandfather, George LaBrande, met my grandmother Molly as a widower and it was from this second union that my mother was born.

Marjorie had a tough life. When she was twelve years old her mother, Molly, died. A couple of weeks later, her father, George, left, and she never saw or heard from him again (however, he was seen across the street from the church while my parents were being married). Marjorie was taken in by her Aunt Maud, who took excellent care of my mother. In the 1970s we received a phone call from Minnesota saying that George had died. He was about ninety-five.

My father, Walter Jerome Starr, met Marjorie at the University of Minnesota where they were students. Both Walter and Marjorie were born in 1910 in St. Paul.

Always interested in flying, my father joined the Minnesota Army Air National Guard and flew planes in WWI, continuing through 1939, the year he and my mother were married. After retiring from the National Guard, my dad worked for his brother, who owned five typewriter stores in St. Paul, then my father worked at Brown and Bigelow, a calendar company in Indiana. He came back to St. Paul and took a job with the International Milling Company, producing Robin Hood Flour, a fairly famous brand at the time. The company was in major competition with Pillsbury and General Mills.

Peter was actually born in La Crosse, Wisconsin because International Milling had transferred my father, and thus me and my pregnant mother, there for a while. After Peter was born, we moved back to Minnesota and lived with my father's mother. I have some vivid memories of that time, like having to shovel coal from the coal chute into the furnace. My grandmother had been injured in a bad street car accident, so my slight-of-build mother was down there shoveling coal.

In 1941, Walter found himself a pilot once again, this time in the 109th squadron. At that time, they were reassigning the squadron to Hawaii, but people with families could opt out, which he did, though it made him subject to the draft. Had he gone to Honolulu in 1941, who's to say whether or not he would have been killed in the attack on Pearl Harbor? After Peter's birthday and Pearl Harbor, he continued with the milling company for two years because of the number of children he had (three of us were underfoot by then), but he was finally drafted in 1943. Apparently they didn't recognize his National Guard service, and my dad was no longer an officer.

My brother Walter John Starr was born in St. Paul on July 28, 1945. We always called him John. As it happened, he and I were both in the Air Force about the same time in the mid-1960s. He flew out of Charleston, South Carolina with the Military Aircraft Command and flew cargo into Tan Son Nhut Air Base during the Vietnam War. He was also a qualified nuclear weapons safety officer and we always wondered why they needed one of those. He got involved in radio when he was stationed in Charleston.

After the war ended, people were coming out of the service quickly, but our father didn't come home until the end of 1946. That's when he told me about being trained as a pilot to fly B-29s to fly over a target and drop *one* bomb. You would immediately think Hiroshima or Nagasaki, that my dad might have had a hand in ending the war, but I finally found out for sure when my first cousin, Ed Starr, obtained the records of the 109th Squadron. My father was not chosen to drop Little Boy or Fat Man on the Japanese.

In 1946 we moved to Wausau, Wisconsin and lived there for five years. When I was eight years old, Paul Joseph Starr was born in Rothschild, Wisconsin in May of 1948.

In 1950 it was back to Minneapolis. The three oldest Starr boys entered St. Thomas Elementary School. Peter was always doing little things to make money and at the end of every day, he would put some dimes in his fishing box. I remember that, for some reason, older kids made Peter and me run into oncoming traffic to scoop up dimes. Confronting danger was part of our early lives as, I guess, it was later on.

We boys spent a lot of our free time together, fishing, sailing, going to the ten day Aquatennial in Minneapolis and the Twin Cities Winter Carnival.

It was the best of times.

By 1950, our father was the Midwest manager for the International Milling Company, but in 1952, he was promoted to national sales manager of the whole company, working in New York City. That was the one job he had that really changed my life because I was now on the East Coast, went to Eastern schools, and met different kinds of people than I had ever encountered before. For a guy who didn't have a college degree, my father did pretty well and he read a lot.

I Liked "Ike"

In 1952, when we were still living in Minnesota, I volunteered to help with the state's Eisenhower campaign. World War II hero General Dwight David Eisenhower ran as a Republican, not with a message but rather as the guy who won the war and was going to do some great things for America. I was just eleven years old, and the youngest Eisenhower volunteer in the country, which brought the attention of *Life* magazine. They wrote a story about me in the March 31st issue, a national story, and I remember standing in the Minneapolis airport when a man reading the magazine looked at me and asked, "Are you the guy in this picture?"

Although Eisenhower came in second in the Minnesota GOP primary—to the ever-popular former Minnesota governor and favorite son Harold Stassen (44% to 37%)—"Ike" won the nomination at the national convention and eventually the White House. But the *Life* magazine story was a really big deal and I ended up, at my age, with quite a bit of notoriety in the Republican party.

Meeting Bill Buckley

Whether it was fate or just coincidence, the Buckley family and the Starr family moved to Stamford, Connecticut on the same day in June of 1952. Stamford is a bedroom community of New York City and my dad bought a house there, commuting every day to the City.

Here Peter, John, and Paul were in one school, St. Mary's, and I in another, Rogers Junior High. I still campaigned for Eisenhower and had a lot of dealings with George H. W. Bush's father, Prescott Bush, who was a U.S. Senator. I even got to meet Richard Nixon, also a U.S. Senator, on a campaign stop in Connecticut and took a train ride with him. I was really into politics at that age.

Peter and I got jobs as paperboys, and that's how we met the great William F. Buckley, Jr. To us, it was just amazing. We had these huge bicycle baskets and Pete had one route while I had another. His route serviced the island Wallack's Point, where Buckley lived, as well as Rock and Roll legend Alan Freed. My route included what became the "silent majority," a really isolated section of Stamford with a gate keeper.

As paperboys we were paid $6.15 a week and we had to deliver 130 newspapers every day, all over Stamford. Imagine being out there in all kinds of weather, all times of the year for $6.15 a *week*, covering a fairly large amount of geography in our community. We lived on a place called Shippan Point. Both our area and Buckley's neighborhood on Wallack's Point were connected by land but when we had big hurricanes, as we did in those years, a lot of times we were just cut off. If we were out on Shippan Point, that's where we were. I remember times when we got trapped in downtown Stamford when it flooded and Buckley had the same problem at Wallack's Point.

We didn't realize what a big celebrity Buckley was at the time. In 1951, he had just finished a book called *God and Man at Yale*, wrote newspaper columns, and was the budding Thomas Jefferson of the "pulled-together" Republican party after the defeat of the Republicans at the hands of Harry Truman in 1948. Bill and others were instrumental in Eisenhower's presidential win in 1952.

At the time, we didn't know exactly what it was Buckley did, but he was helping organize and unite the party again and developed a conservative marching song, so to speak, to make a big appeal to the public as a conservative entity. Eisenhower's support consisted of a lot of moderate Republicans from the East Coast. He won two big elections, in 1952 and 1956, but it was not so much on theory and politics as it was that he was "Ike" Eisenhower, the American war hero. After him, the Republicans had to develop a candidate and a philosophy that was not built around one famous candidate with a hell of a track record. You don't really beat a title like WWII's victorious Supreme Commander of the Allied forces in Europe. All of this developed into Nixon's first run for president, against John Kennedy in 1960. Nixon was not as good a candidate then as he proved to be later, and he lost that election very narrowly.

Although Buckley was on Peter's paper route, we covered for each other quite a bit, and so I got to know Buckley too. But Peter had the better and longer relationship with him. I remember I called him Mr. Buckley, but there was finally a point in time when he said, "Oh, just call me Bill," and I thought, *Wow. That's really a big deal.*

In the beginning, I think Buckley was much more impressed with Peter, but he was impressed with some of the writing I had done, and he used to come over to the house when we lived in at 71 Fairview Avenue in Stamford. Buckley would come over and pick up Peter, and he would take time to visit with our mom and dad for a little bit. Peter regularly did things with Bill, including learning how to sail and taking care of Bill's boats, and I helped or went along with Peter more intermittently.

Some years later, Buckley took up painting and he painted a portrait of Peter and took it over to my parents' house. I still have it. My brother Paul and I always thought it was terrible by anybody's standards, but mom and dad treasured it because Bill had painted it. I always thought it looked like a "paint by the numbers" project. It had a likeness of Peter, it just wasn't great.

In 1954, I entered St. Basil's Ukraine Seminary Prep School in Stamford, graduating in 1958. Peter joined me there in 1956, graduating in 1960. You could always spot the Starrs at St Basil's. Mother dressed Pete and me the same. You could get away with that in elementary school but not in high school. Still, our mother chose identical clothes, which set us up for special treatment. St. Basil's was a life-defining educational experience because it provided what, in those days, was called "a classical education." Subjects included Latin, English Literature, the sciences, and advanced math. It was designed to prepare a young person for succeeding in life.

In 1958, Peter and I were split up geographically. Pete continued high school at St. Basil's, also spending more time with Bill. But in summers we were together again, and I got to see our gang of mutual friends, one of whom is now Governor of Connecticut, Dannel Patrick "Dan" Malloy.

Peter and Bill and the Boats

Buckley's Cruiser Missing

STAMFORD (UPI)—The Coast Guard has been asked to be on the lookout for the 42-foot cutter "Tanic" [sic], owned by author William F. Buckley, Jr. The craft, with three men aboard, left St. Johns, N.B., Tuesday, but has been unreported since that time, according to Buckley. He said the skipper, Peter Star [sic] of Stamford, had been slated to contact him Wednesday to report his position, but failed....The Coast Guard said Star [sic] may have put into port along the way to avoid Hurricane Cleo. Buckley said he "wasn't surprised" that Star [sic] failed to call. He said the craft isn't due back until next week.[2]

I asked one of my brothers to share this story from his perspective.
John Starr:

When I first met Bill Buckley he was really young, I would say thirty. And Peter was the captain of his sailing vessel. So, Peter hired me to work on the boat and do the grunt work. The first boat was called *The Panic*, a steel-hulled sloop with a level indicator to measure how much the boat was tilting in the water, and Buckley had made a marking at a certain angle of tilt which read, "Patsy gets off." Patsy was his wife.

In 1960, I was working at a Boy Scout camp for the summer. There was only one phone in the whole camp. Someone came and told me that there was a very important phone call for me up at the office and I needed to get up there right away and take the call. I was thinking there might have been a car wreck or something like that. I got up there and picked up the phone and it was my mother, and she said "John, I have terrible news. Your brother has been lost at sea. He was sailing on *The Panic* up around Cape Cod and he's missing. He didn't show up where he was supposed to show up."

Well, he made it safely back to Stamford and I got home myself. When I finally saw Peter, he told me, "John, we had this pea soup fog. We couldn't see anything and we had no idea where we were, so I just weighed anchor and decided to wait out the fog.

It was scary as hell because we would hear these huge fog horns and all of a sudden a huge ship would go by us. We were scared to death because we were in some kind of shipping lane, and we were afraid we were going to get run over. Sometimes we could see the lights of these vessels going by us and they were high up in the air, so they were big freighters or something with topsides about 60 feet high, and we were only three our four feet above the water."

The Panic was pretty much scuttled in 1961 during another hurricane, so Buckley got another one called *The Suzy Wong*, a sailboat built in Hong Kong. It was absolutely gorgeous. It was hand-carved below deck, made of beautiful teakwood, which requires a tremendous amount of maintenance. So, my job was to keep the teak looking good. I would take steel wool and cleanser and literally scrub the decks. When you did it well, the decks would have a beautiful look to them. I'm working on the boat one day, scrubbing with the steel wool, cutting up my hands, and here's Bill Buckley. He introduced himself and he was just as nice and friendly and gracious as could be. I knew the man was from a very wealthy family and I was very pleasantly surprised by his down-to-earth personality. The only thing I remember about him at that time was that he used vocabulary that was beyond me. I was about thirteen or fourteen years old at the time.

There was one more boat that played an important role in the Starr–Buckley Saga. It was called *The Cyrano*, and it would play its part fifteen years later.

For our family in the late 1950s, we were sitting in a budding national recession and our dad was out of work.

It was the worst of times.

The college education had to be cheap. I found a small Catholic University, St. Francis College (now St. Francis University) in Loretto, Pennsylvania. I had offers from UVA and George Washington, but we just didn't have the money.

Dad paid the first semester at St. Francis. When the second semester came around, I didn't have enough money to pay the tuition. But, because I had all A's the first semester, the school finally awarded me a tuition scholarship and I made up the financial difference by working in the college dining hall. I wasn't allowed eat there, though. I was thrown out several times for doing so, and it was really tough to see all my friends and fraternity brothers at the "slop" window all semester.

Instead, I spent fifty cents a day for a steak sandwich with money I was paid to be a fraternity officer, President of the Tau Kappa Epsilon (TKE) chapter, Delta Phi. My opponent in that race, by the way, was a chap named James Buchanan. His older brother is conservative television commentator and occasional candidate for the White House, Pat Buchanan.

One of my favorite pals at St. Francis, Thaddeus (Ted) Wojtusik, from Connecticut, had a favorite saying: "If you can't go Greek, go Teek." He also liked to point out that we TKEs were the only non-alcoholic chapter on campus. That may explain why we weren't the largest chapter on campus.

I graduated St. Francis Summa Cum Laude in 1962. Peter and I went to my St. Francis graduation together. We were late and I had to join the line in progress. That same year I went to Georgetown Law School in Washington, D.C. on a scholarship. I also got a fellowship and eventually I earned a bachelor's, a master's, and a doctorate degree.

Peter used to come visit me at St. Francis and in D.C. Every car I owned in those years had expired licenses so we stopped at state lines to change plates from our library of ones in the trunk. I visited Peter at Georgetown, where he attended, and we continued to have great times together. I went to his graduation from Georgetown, then Peter moved back to Stamford and remained there until 1964.

Chapter 2

Freedom Summer

My Journalistic Debut

In 1961, after the Bay of Pigs fiasco of April 15-19 when Cuban exiles tried to oust their leader Fidel Castro with US backing, I wrote what would be called today an "op-ed" piece in the *Stamford Advocate*. I wrote that it was a delusion for the US to think we could send tractors to Cuba to help liberate the Bay of Pigs prisoners. I thought it was a sellout to the Communists, but the plan eventually worked... sort of.

Castro demanded in mid-May of 1961 that the United States give him 500 bulldozer/tractors at a cost of about 28 million dollars in return for the release of more than 1100 prisoners. A group of private citizens, among them former First Lady Eleanor Roosevelt, formed a committee called "Tractors for Freedom," to raise the money. About a month later negotiations with Castro fell apart and the committee basically disbanded.

Today, many Americans remember the talks as successful and note that the prisoners were soon released in return for the tractors. However, it was actually not until December of 1962, *after* the Cuban Missile Crisis, that an agreement was reached and the slow release of the prisoners began. Castro received not tractors, but about sixty million dollars in food and medicine. [3]

After my article condemning the tractor deal appeared in the *Advocate* in 1961, Buckley asked Peter, "Does your brother always write that well?"

Trouble in the South

In 1964, I was going into my last year at Georgetown before earning my law degree. The school was quite liberal and some of the professors were recruiting people to go to Mississippi to take part in what was being called "Freedom Summer," a dangerous but important project designed to increase black voter registration in the South.

Over the years, I've heard a lot of people confuse the Freedom Summer volunteers of 1964 with the Freedom Riders of 1961. The latter rode Trailways and Greyhound buses from the north and, for their efforts, were brutally beaten at the hands of southern mobs with the encouragement of local law enforcement. One of the buses was even firebombed. The volunteers of '64 were not Riders, nor were they members of the sit-ins of 1960 that finally forced the integration of lunch counters at Woolworth stores in North Carolina.

At that time, the Law Students Civil Rights Research Council based in Washington, D.C. was supporting Freedom Summer. A Georgetown professor submitted my name to them and they wanted me to work in Jackson, Mississippi. While there, I lived on the money I had earned for the next year's classes, which was a little bit of a tough arrangement for me. Still, I had never really been in the South, but I had seen the news on TV with the dogs and fire hoses being used against unarmed people, and I thought *what the hell.*

I was appointed to the headquarters of the National Lawyers Guild, basically the black ABA, in Jackson. The Guild put together a thick, legal page-sized "brochure on Mississippi law relating to Civil Rights and Constitutional Guarantees," and passed copies of it out to the lawyers (and law students, like me), who were going south for the summer. The brochure contained information that lawyers would need to represent anyone, "white or negro," arrested by local author-ities. It had forms and applications for attempts to quash indictments, appeal convictions, and plead poverty to avoid paying court fees. The Guild was determined to fight for the legal rights of blacks all over the U.S but the problem was biggest in the South:

> Virtually the entire bar in the South has refused to give legal repre-
> sentation to Negroes and their white supporters in their historic

drive for full equality... more than 2 million people who reside in Mississippi, a state with more than 2,000 lawyers, can turn to only three (Negro) attorneys who will accept civil rights cases.[4]

I was the only one going from Georgetown but I joined a group of three other guys and we decided to all drive down together to Meridian, Mississippi. Along the way, everything was segregated and, despite everything I'd heard, I was surprised by it: no integrated eating facilities, no integrated bathrooms or hotels. And, because there were two whites and two blacks in our car, the Citizen Councils in these towns, which were a lot like the Klan, took particular note of us. Some of these people were also law enforcement officers with high speed cars.

We couldn't stay in a hotel or anything like it, and I remember stopping in Richmond. We realized we couldn't eat together so we went into a park, just to be out of the car while we ate, not understanding that we shouldn't have been in a park either. It was a very hostile scene, but we ate and just continued our way south.

There was another group working the area at the time called the Council of Federated Organizations (COFO), an umbrella organization for the various entities that had individuals in the field for Freedom Summer. When we got to Meridian (June 20, 1964) we went to the COFO office. It just happened to be the same day Michael Schwerner and Andrew Goodman, two young white men from New York City, and James Chaney, a black man from Meridian, disappeared. They hadn't come back from a trip to Philadelphia, Mississippi to investigate the burning of a church and all three were Freedom Summer volunteers.

When we arrived, Rita Schwerner, wife of the missing Michael, was at COFO waiting for news. Everybody was sitting around, anxious. It got to be later and later. Eventually, everyone realized they weren't going to be coming back, so the next morning we four drove up to Philadelphia in Neshoba County and confronted the sheriff, Lawrence Rainey, on the courthouse steps. Talk about a hostile atmosphere. Some of these Neshoba Country men started beating up the reporters. The FBI was there, hiding around the corners, but they never intervened. This is 1964, Johnson was president, Bobby Kennedy was still at the Justice Department, but the fact is they effectively didn't put anybody in the field. The ones we saw, who we knew to be FBI people, did not intervene in any way and, if we had been set upon by thugs, we'd have been on our own.

The thing to remember is that 1964 was the year the Civil Rights Act passed. President John F. Kennedy had proposed the bill the year before, hoping to give all Americans—regardless of race, color, religion, sex, or national origin—"the right to be served in facilities which are open to the public—hotels, restaurants, theaters, retail stores, and similar establishments." Theoretically, the bill would also protect all Americans' right to vote. President Johnson signed the bill into law on July 2, just eleven days after the murders of Schwerner, Chaney, and Goodman.

The bodies of the three men were finally discovered on August 4, 1964. State and local officials never charged anyone in the killings, but seven men, all of them members of the Ku Klux Klan, were convicted by the Federal government of conspiracy to violate the civil rights of the three victims in December of 1967. None of the men served more than more than six years.

One of my jobs was to go to the Jackson airport and pick up a group of northern lawyers who were going to work in Mississippi for two weeks. We stayed in safe houses as I took them around the state, trying to secure releases for people who had been arrested for trying to vote. The places we stayed had mattresses propped up against the windows. There were guns. There were mobs. It was a very dangerous situation.

I stayed the whole summer and, at the end of it, we were all asked to give affidavits of our activity for inclusion in a book called *Mississippi Black Paper*, published in 1965. Out of 257 submissions, mine was one of the fifty-seven chosen for the book. This is just a portion of my contribution, explaining the burning of the Mt. Zion church, the investigation of which brought the three Freedom Summer volunteers to Neshoba County:

From June 29 to July 25... I participated in an extensive investigation of the destruction of the Mt. Zion Methodist Church, in Philadelphia, Mississippi, and the disappearance of three civil rights workers in that same community. At Mt. Zion, Tuesday nights were traditionally set aside for the leaders and stewards meeting. On those nights church business was disposed of and the collection for the pastor was taken... [On the evening of June 16, 1964] There were approximately ten people in attendance.... The business was concluded about 10 pm and those in attendance began to leave the church. As they emerged from the church they noticed three strange vehicles in the church parking lot. In addition to that, twenty-five to thirty men, all armed, had formed a single line between the road and the church....

The Mt. Zion members passed by these men and headed to their cars and trucks to return home.... Some people proceeded north on Longdale Road to get to their homes, while others turned to the South. As the South group... was proceeding home... they were forced to the side of the road by a pick-up truck. Five or six white men approached the Mt. Zion vehicles and ordered the occupants to turn off their lights. The people were then forcibly pulled out of their car and truck and questioned. With one exception all the people who went the South route were beaten, either with fists or, as in one case, a heavy blunt instrument....

One man who lives in that area noticed a glow in the area of the church between twelve and one in the morning...Another local resident was awakened by a car outside his house at approximately two o'clock. As he looked to see what the car was doing he noticed a glow in the sky in the vicinity of the church.

At the church site itself all that is now to be seen are a few bricks and some twisted metal roofing lying where it fell... The church itself was located in a heavily wooded area and it seems that a fire the size of the one that engulfed Mt. Zion Church should have spread. But it did not, which gives rise to the impression that it was tended so it would not.

Signed, Michael F. Starr[5]

After the *Mississippi Black Paper* was published, I was invited to be a guest on David Susskind's national TV show, "Open End," and I lectured at a couple of universities. Some of the movies that have been made tell an entirely different story of what had actually happened. "Mississippi Burning" (1988) with Gene Hackman was one of them. William Bradford Huie wrote *Three Lives for Mississippi*, and he interviewed me for the book.

In 1988, I was named chairman of the Radio TV department at the University of Southern Illinois. The department was rated number one in the country at one point when I was the Chair and one of my professors was a black lady from Chicago, Judith McCray. When I told her about Freedom Summer, she said, "Let's do a documentary about it." We persuaded Ossie Davis and Ruby Dee to narrate it and the technical crew was made up of students and people otherwise associated with the university. We licensed *Mississippi, America* to PBS and all the proceeds have gone to scholarship funds.

Due to renewed publicity, in 2005 Klansman Edgar Ray Killen was convicted of three counts of manslaughter and was sentenced to a total of sixty years in prison. The interesting thing is that he was convicted by a Mississippi jury in Neshoba County, not a Federal court.

Even during the Freedom Summer, there was a lot of talk about the possibility of someone assassinating Dr. King. I kept telling my parents and other people about the rumors I'd heard. Some of these people said, "Maybe that would be a good result." I said, "You are going to rue the day that Martin Luther King gets assassinated and we have to deal with the consequences." I thought King was doing the right thing and it's amazing to me that a lot more people weren't killed or maimed for life during that struggle.

I never met King. I did not go to the March in Washington in 1963. To me, with the civil rights struggle, it didn't matter if you were a Democrat or a Republican. I saw it as a very big Constitutional issue, and that had to be resolved through King's policies and a lot of court cases. I didn't see it as a political football at the time, although it ended up that way. How you could not say that King was attempting to lead us in a new direction?

After Starr Broadcasting was formed, we happened to buy three black radio stations. My experience in the South actually helped us gain approval for this purchase from the Federal Communications Committee (FCC) and my days in Mississippi also had an impact on how we ran those stations.

The 1964 National Conventions

It was just sort of a gala. Everybody knew that the GOP nominee, Barry Goldwater, was going to lose in November. No way was he going to beat Lyndon Johnson, but they thought that this was the beginning point of a "re-started" Republican Party, which held the convention at Cow Palace in San Francisco. Buckley, Peter, and I all attended and it was a very exciting time. We got to see Barry make his famous "extremism in defense of Liberty is no vice" speech, and we got to see liberal Republican Nelson Rockefeller almost booed off the stage.

After that we went to the Democratic National Convention in Atlantic City, which was exciting too, but not for the same reasons. The regular Democratic Party delegates from Mississippi had been elected without the participation of blacks in the state, and the Freedom Democratic Party was formed in an effort to have the Regulars ousted from the convention on national television. Lyndon Johnson, who was about to be coronated at the convention, wanted no part of that. He knew that if the Mississippi blacks were seated, the other white delegations would storm out of the convention. The Freedom Democrats were told they could have two delegates seated on the floor to observe, but they could not vote. The Freedom Democrats said thanks but no thanks, and left the convention. But they had put the spotlight on what was going on in the South, and the next year Congress passed the Voting Rights Act of 1965.

I had just come back from Mississippi and Freedom Summer and Peter, Buckley, and I were walking down the Boardwalk, passing a bunch of the Freedom Democratic Party people on the street. They were all yelling to me! Buckley asked, "How do you know all those people?" I just smiled and said that I was recently on special assignment in Mississippi.

Despite all the exciting things happening, I wanted to leave the convention because I had a girl in Connecticut that I was getting engaged to, but Buckley insisted that I stay. He kept me out of what would have been a very bad marriage.

In 1965, I was blasted in the Congressional Record by Senator James Eastland of Mississippi. He entered the names of the lawyers, like myself, who had attended Freedom Summer in his state into the Record, and he called us Communists on the Senate floor. Eastland, interestingly, was a former law partner and a good friend of William Cox, the judge who was to preside over the 1967 federal trial that convicted the Klansmen. As a result of Eastland's actions, I was unable to secure any legal employment in D.C., where I had graduated from Georgetown that same year. I was out of options, so I went to Omaha to work for my neighbor William F. Buckley.

Chapter 3

Profile—Who Was William F. Buckley?

It's possible that you, reading this in the twenty-first century, may not know exactly who Bill Buckley was and what influence he had on twentieth-century America. If you don't already have an idea of just how or why William F. Buckley was famous (or, to many, infamous), this chapter will provide a short profile to that purpose.

They say that no man is a hero to his butler. We were not exactly his butlers, but eventually that saying was to become, sadly, so true. Still, to my brother Peter and me, as youngsters, Buckley was our hero.

Frank...Not Francis!

Early in his life, William F. Buckley, Jr. showed the world he was not to be messed with. He was born in New York City as William *Francis* on November 24, 1925. His father's middle name was Frank, and mom and dad wanted a Junior. The family priest, however, made it clear that baby Bill must have a Saint's name, so he was christened William Francis Buckley. No Junior. According to family legend, when he was five years old, Bill demanded that his name be changed to "Frank" like his father's. They did so and the world had to deal with William F. Buckley, *Junior.* [6]

William Frank Buckley, *Senior* (whose parents had both immigrated from Ireland through Canada), was born in 1881 in Washington-on-the-Brazos, Texas.[7] His family called him Will. He moved to Mexico in 1908 and started a small law firm, but his wealth came later from the oil drilling business in Mexico and Venezuela. Will married the beautiful Aloïse Josephine Antonia Steiner, a native of New Orleans in 1917.

In those days there was a revolution-a-minute in Mexico, and in 1921, four years after he and Aloïse were married, Will backed the wrong side of a revolution and was kicked out of the country.[8] He moved his oil company to Venezuela in 1924, but didn't strike oil until 1939.

Buckley had nine siblings: Aloïse, John, Priscilla, James, Jane, Patricia, Fergus ("Reid"), Maureen, and Carol. Most people say Reid could have been Bill's twin. It was Reid who wrote a memoir shortly after Buckley died in 2008, entitled *An American Family: The Buckleys*. In the book, Reid tells how Will Buckley made his oil fortune and how Will's father, Sheriff John, was a close friend of Pat Garrett, the man who shot and killed Billy the Kid.[9] But, according to Reid, Will Buckley had his own link to wild west history. When Will was escorting the payroll of a large American company by train, he was confronted by the revolutionary gang of Pancho Villa, who told the conductor that he would shoot him if the conductor didn't turn over the payroll. Will spoke up, saying that he, himself, had hidden the money and Villa would have to deal with him if he wanted it. According to the story, Pancho was impressed enough to let the conductor live, and he asked Will Buckley to come see him sometime.[10]

Bill Buckley spoke English as a third language, which he learned at age seven after Spanish and French, the latter of which he learned when he attended a school in Paris. He also attended high school at Beaumont Preparatory College in England. When in the United States, the Buckley family lived in Sharon, Connecticut in a house called Great Elm, and spent their summers in Camden, South Carolina.[11] Bill's interests included sailing, riding, hunting, and music, including "the instrument I love beyond all others," the harpsichord, which he played until the end of his life.[12]

God and Bill at Yale

On April 13, 1945, as a member of the U.S. Army stationed at Fort Benning, Georgia, Bill found himself in Warm Springs as part of the honor guard that followed Eleanor Roosevelt and the hearse carrying the casket of her husband Franklin to the funeral train for the ride north to Washington, D.C. Considering Bill's deeply conservative political views, I've sometimes wondered if he might have participated in the honor guard under protest. [13]

After the war was over, Bill entered Yale University and joined several politically conservative organizations, including the very secret Skull and Bones Society. That society, at the time, mostly consisted of white, Protestant men. Buckley, the raging Catholic (he once wanted to be a priest), was accepted nonetheless, but their sense of diversity did not include the inclusion of women.[14] In 1992, as an alumnus, Buckley helped to obtain a temporary restraining order to block a move to admit women, but the lawsuit was eventually dropped and women were admitted for the first time that year.[15]

By his 1950 graduation from Yale, Bill had met and married his sister Pat's Vassar College roommate, who was also named Pat.[16] Patricia Aldyen Austin Taylor and Bill were married until her death in 2007 at the age of 80. Interestingly enough, while Bill's parents had ten children, and his grandfather, Sheriff John, had eight, Pat and Bill Buckley only had one child, a son named Christopher, who is a well-known writer and humorist.[17]

The year after he graduated, Bill earned his first taste of national publicity by writing and publishing a book about his school days, a diatribe against his alma mater called *God and Man at Yale*.[18] According to his obituary in the *New York Times*, he wrote the book because he had been replaced as the main speaker for Yale's Alumni Day celebration due to his constant criticism of the school. The *Times* also reported that the book attracted notice only because Buckley gave $10,000 to his publisher for the book's advertizing.

Controversial because Buckley claimed that Yale was forcing liberal ideas on its students, *God and Man at Yale* even named names and called for some professors to be fired.[19] The Roman Catholic Buckley basically accused Yale, and other universities, of kicking God off campus. When he was invited back to Yale to receive an honorary degree in 2000, he said, "It's true. God has finally returned to Yale."

The CIA and Howard Hunt

God and Man at Yale was the first of a total of fifty-six books that Buckley would write over his career, eleven of them spy novels. The spy thrillers almost certainly had their origins in 1951, when Buckley briefly worked for the Central Intelligence Agency.

In that same year, Buckley met E. Howard Hunt, who would later become famous as one of the ringleaders of the 1972 Watergate scandal, when Republican officials arranged a break-in at the Democratic National Headquarters in the Watergate office complex in D.C.

In the forward to Hunt's 2007 memoir, *American Spy*, which was published just two months after Hunt died, Buckley wrote that he was working as a deep-cover agent and was told to report to Hunt at the U.S. Embassy in Mexico City, where Hunt assigned him to do some translating from Spanish into English. Buckley wrote in the forward that the two became friends. Apparently, not long before Hunt was supposed to go to jail for his part in the Watergate caper, he "startled" Buckley by telling him he was going to disclose everything he knew about Watergate, including a plan to assassinate columnist Jack Anderson, "if the high command at the Nixon White House thought this necessary."[20]

Apparently the White House thought better of that plan, but it was too late for Richard Nixon, who resigned his Presidency in 1974 after losing all of his support in Congress because of the scandal and cover-up.

The National Review

Bill started *National Review* magazine in 1955 with about $300,000 from friends and a $100,000 gift from his father.[21] In the first issue, Buckley stated his objective: *[The National Review] stands athwart history, yelling Stop....*[22]

While most Republicans in America were yelling "I like Ike,"[23] *National Review* supported Dwight Eisenhower's re-election in 1956 with the lukewarm statement: "The danger posed by the Republican Party today, lies bare-breasted in its universal emblem, I Like Ike. It should read, I prefer Ike."

In 1964, the magazine supported Barry Goldwater for president. In fact, it was Buckley's brother-in-law L. Brent Bozell, Jr. who ghost-wrote *The Conscience of a Conservative* for Goldwater. Bozell married the same sister, Patricia Buckley, who had introduced Bill to his own wife Patricia Taylor. [24]

Over the years, Buckley backtracked on the magazine's original segregationist viewpoint. After Buckley's death, a writer named Sam Tanenhaus (remember that name), produced a Q & A piece for the *New York Times*. He said Buckley eventually changed his opposition to the civil rights movement, admitting it was a mistake for *National Review* to have opposed the Civil Rights Act of 1964 and the Voting Rights Act of 1965. Buckley later endorsed the move to make Martin Luther King, Jr.'s birthday a federal holiday.[25]

Another name to remember from *National Review* is that of William Rusher, who served as publisher from 1957 to 1988. He helped Buckley start Young Americans for Freedom in 1960. He founded the "Draft Goldwater" movement, which was well publicized in *National Review*, and he opposed Richard Nixon for president in 1972 because of Nixon's policies on China.[26]

When *National Review* celebrated its 25th anniversary in 1980, Rusher stated "I think this is the watershed moment. Conservatism is at the crossroads. And incidentally, our old enemy liberalism has died."

Rusher, himself, died at the age of 87 in 2011.

The most important thing about *National Review* is that it was the basis of the conservative movement that we all know today. Just as Buckley opposed the far right John Birch Society and "other kooks," he might well feel the same way about the Tea Party of the twenty-first century. Hugh Kenner, who wrote for *National Review* said, "Without Bill...there probably would be no respectable conservative movement in this country."[27]

Reagan Snubs Bill on the 25th Anniversary of *National Review*

To many people, Richard Nixon was not a real conservative, so he wanted to gain credibility amongst deep conservatives by having Buckley visit the White House and talk over various policy matters. Bill used to go and see him quite a bit. Reagan, on the other hand, did not need Buckley. So when it was clear that Reagan was going to be the nominee, then president, Bill invited him to be the guest speaker at the 25th anniversary of *National Review*, scheduled for December of 1980. Reagan agreed but he did not show up.

Buckley went nuts. He was on the phone, on the phone, on the phone. He couldn't believe Reagan was going to stiff him like that, but he did. The Associated Press ran this headline: *Reagan snubs "Cinderella"—misses party.* It was an awful thing.

Why did Reagan do it? I think some of his political advisors thought Reagan didn't need to spend any more time with Buckley when he had the presidency wrapped up. There was no sense in being known for spending time with a looney.

Buckley had his own explanation. He said that Reagan had accepted the invitation to speak and requested a reminder before the event. Bill did so by telegram, signing it, for some reason, "Cinderella."

The AP report said, "That bit of whimsy caused Reagan's aides to route the telegram either to the wastebasket or security people—it wasn't clear which—instead of to the President-elect's scheduling office. By the time the mix-up was discovered, Reagan was already booked [elsewhere] for the night."[28]

His associates recalled there was hell to pay that night. Buckley was absolutely and awfully offended. Furthermore, where do you come up with a quality speaker at the last minute? I can't recall if he got anybody or not.

Reagan actually did show up to speak at the 30th anniversary dinner in 1985, but I'm sure it wasn't quite the same.

Another reason to remember *National Review* is that, without it, Buckley could not have needed money to save it. Thus, he might not have bought a radio station in Omaha, there might not have been a Starr Broadcasting, and this book might not have been necessary.

The Conservative Party

Nineteen sixty-two saw the creation of a third political party, by a man named J. Daniel Mahoney.[29] He thought the governor of New York, Nelson Rockefeller, was too liberal so he founded the Conservative Party, which grew strong in the state of New York but not nationwide. However, it was strong enough to persuade Bill Buckley to run for mayor of New York City in 1965. He ran on the new Conservative Party ticket so he could take votes away from Republican John Lindsay, also on the Liberal Party line on the ballot. There was no way Buckley could win, and when a reporter asked him what he would do if he actually won the election, Buckley said, "Demand a recount."[30] Incidentally, J. Daniel Mahoney became Bill Buckley's personal attorney and figured prominently in the downfall of the brothers Starr.

The Conservative Party of New York however, had one last fling in the limelight when it sent Bill Buckley's brother, James, to the U.S. Senate in 1970. Most likely he would not have won if the original incumbent, Robert F. Kennedy, had run for re-election instead of for president, and had not been assassinated in June of 1968.[31]

Before he joined Peter and I at Starr Broadcasting, our brother Paul volunteered for the Buckley for Senate campaign. Peter actually paid Paul for his work (yes, I know), which was Peter's contribution to the campaign. For three months Paul worked in the Buckley family oil company building in Manhattan. Jim, Reid, and John Buckley were there every day and Paul got to know all of them.

"The one person you never saw there," said Paul, "was Bill Buckley. In a sense I knew the other three Buckley's better than I did Bill. He probably barely knew my name. In later years he might not have even remembered me. I was Peter's little brother."

The Republican in the 1970 senate race was Congressman Charles Goodell (father of current NFL Commissioner Roger Goodell), who was appointed by Governor Rockefeller after Bobby Kennedy was killed. In 1976, Jim Buckley ran for re-election as a Republican and lost to Democrat Daniel Patrick Moynihan.[32]

Feud with Gore Vidal

Buckley was well known for his long-running feud with liberal writer and political debater Gore Vidal. Vidal had more literary "hits" than Buckley, writing not only novels but biographies, stage plays, and screenplays.[33] Among his most prominent works are *Suddenly, Last Summer* (screenplay) and *The Best Man* (stage play and screenplay). Many of his works, including those two, deal with homosexuality. Vidal himself had a relationship with Howard Austen that lasted fifty-three years, until Austen's death.[34] But Vidal claimed the two never had a physical relationship. He also said that "everyone is bisexual."[35] After Vidal's death in 2012 at the age of 86, his nephew Burr Steers said in an interview with the *New York Times* that his uncle feared that William F. Buckley had a file on him that may have included evidence of Vidal's involvement with underage boys. "I know Buckley had a file on him that Gore feared," said Steers in the article. "It would make sense if that material was about him having underage sex."[36]

Their rivalry boiled over in the famous face-off between the two men in 1968 during a debate on ABC-TV at the Democratic National Convention in Chicago. While the helpless moderator, Howard K. Smith, looked on in apparent horror, Vidal called Buckley a "crypto-Nazi." Enraged, Buckley raised himself out of his chair and said to Vidal, "Now listen, you *queer*, stop calling me a crypto-Nazi or I'll sock you in your goddamned face and you'll stay plastered." Pretty racy stuff for 1968 network television, and it was all "live" with no bleeps.[37]

After both men wrote essays about the incident in *Esquire* magazine, they traded libel lawsuits back and forth for the next couple of years. Eventually the suits were dropped, but Buckley obtained an apology from *Esquire* as part of the settlement.

Firing Line

In 1966, Bill started his conservative television program *Firing Line*. It began as a local program on WOR-TV in New York, and then was syndicated nationwide by RKO General. In 1971, the hour-long show (including commercials) moved to and stayed on PBS until December, 1999. At that time it was the longest-running program on television with the same host throughout. In fact, more people probably know Buckley from *Firing Line* than from any of his other work.[38]

The original concept was for Bill to debate a liberal each week. Simple as that. Over the years, of course, his guests included many from the political right as well.[39]

"There was a lot that had been said by *National Review*," Buckley told the *Times*, "that needed to be said face to face to its critics." CNN blogger, Andrew Fergusen wrote, "From Jack Kerouac to Mary McCarthy, and every President from Nixon through Bush, there are few figures of intellectual significance who didn't submit to Buckley's leisurely sparring."[40]

Apparently, the show even turned Bill into a sex symbol. A poll conducted in the '70s by *Psychology Today* reported that "an alarmingly high percentage of women fantasized about Buckley while having sex with their husbands."[41]

Why Did Bill Buckley Talk Like That?

If Buckley had only written books and newspaper and magazine columns, never branching into his TV show, most people would not have known how he spoke. He sounded like nobody else in America. His parents were from the South, but he didn't have a southern accent, just an occasional drawl. He grew up and studied in Mexico, but did not have a Hispanic accent. Nor did his time in Paris seem to influence his speech. He grew up partly in Connecticut and did have what Michelle Tsai of *Slate* called a "Connecticut lockjaw sound." She also used the terms "High Church accent," and "preposterously mellifluous." She emphasized that his gestures made him "prone to caricature. He tended to pause for long stretches, wag his tongue, and open his mouth in an exaggerated way. To emphasize a point, he would make a tent with his fingers or grin as he spoke a key word.[42]

After reading this small profile, you know a little about how America and the world saw him. Read on and you will learn how Peter and I saw William F. Buckley.

Chapter 4

Omaha

I Discover Radio

Peter and I had thought about a broadcast career but we were going to do it ourselves. We had come across broadcast stations in the Virgin Islands, where every young man wants to go anyway. There was a radio-TV station for sale, WIVI, in St. Thomas, and the guy was selling it on paper, so we didn't have to have financing. We thought "that's the deal for us" because we didn't have any money, but then Buckley showed up and said, "I have a radio station in Omaha."

It was called KOWH-660 AM, a 500 watt day-timer, and the call numbers stood for Omaha World Herald. Buckley bought it in 1957 from Todd Storz, who is recognized as the one who "invented" Top Forty radio. Apparently, at the time Storz bought his second station, WTIX-AM 690 in New Orleans, he was listening to WDSU-AM 1280 and they were playing the Top Twenty songs every afternoon. Todd decided that forty was better than twenty, others agreed, and that's how the phrase "Top Forty" was born. KOWH was the first to play a limited song list twenty-four hours a day, but New Orleans is where the words "Top Forty" were first heard on the air. Gordon McLendon of Dallas also claimed credit for "Top Forty", but most say Storz was first.

At that time, Todd Storz was the biggest name in radio. By the time he died in 1964 at the age of thirty-nine, he owned stations in Kansas City, St. Louis, Miami, Minneapolis, and Oklahoma City.

KOWH was little, but it could be heard not only in Nebraska, but in parts of Iowa, South Dakota, Missouri, and Kansas as well. It was not a clear channel station because it was too low-power, but it's low position on the AM dial, 660, gave it longer broadcast waves than at the higher end of the spectrum. Low dial position means a broader signal, so it was able to compete with all the other stations in Omaha during the day.

The station was a big hit all through the early and mid-1950s when Storz owned it, but then a guy named Don Burden took over rival station KOIL-AM, which was a 5,000 watt full-time station (broadcasting during the day and at night) and he copied everything Storz did, even playing Top Forty on his station. That was a problem for KOWH because, as just a day-timer, KOIL had no competition for that format at night. They started beating KOWH in the ratings. Burden even created a promotion campaign with the slogan "KOIL: the station that doesn't run down at sundown."

Faced with these troubles, Storz finally sold KOWH to Bill Buckley in 1957 for a whopping $822,000. Bill bought the station to help subsidize *National Review*, which was losing money. After several years of owning the station, Buckley was still not getting his desired return so he asked Peter and I to go to Omaha to see if some new blood couldn't turn things around. Peter went first.

In 1964, I was at Georgetown Law and Peter had just graduated from Georgetown as an undergrad. He'd even been one of the editors of *Hoya*, the campus newspaper. Bill asked Peter to go to work at KOWH as a salesman and Peter put to use what he'd learned from Buckley, although on a small scale. The local paper thought enough of it to write a small article announcing his arrival. Eventually Peter became sales manager, then general manager.

I was still in law school at Georgetown in the mid-1960s and I had an apartment across from the Capitol. I spent time in the Radio TV gallery at the Capitol, recording congressional proceedings for Peter and the radio station. I followed the Nebraska delegation closely. During that time there was another coup in Saigon, Vietnam, and a new Vietnamese ambassador came to Washington. I called the embassy and I said I wanted to speak to the new ambassador. They put me right through. In an effort to help out Peter, I told the ambassador that I represented part of the midwest United States with this radio station—KOWH—and I would like to do an interview. He said to come right over and I realized I had to go out and get a tape recorder on the way to the embassy. There was one particular lady who had been very helpful to me at the embassy and I thought I would take a bottle of perfume with me. When I got to the embassy I handed the lady the perfume and I looked at the box. It said "Ambush." That was the name of the perfume. Just the right gift for a young lady whose country was in turmoil from presidential coups and foreign fighters.

I realized that, even though I was unqualified, I could do these interviews. But I needed some press cards. Peter sent me a box of cards, and when I opened the box the cards read not KOWH but "Pete's Mill." The printer had made the cards for the wrong client. I figured that if Peter failed in radio, at least he could go into another business—he already had the cards printed.

After I got out of law school in 1965, Peter asked me to come out and join him in Omaha. When I got there, Peter was already the president, I became the executive vice president, and we built this company. At that point we were both established in Omaha, and doing things regularly with Buckley, who would come out and promote the radio station.

Keep in mind that neither of us had any background in radio at all. I had never been in a radio station and neither had Peter. He got his first call from Buckley's accountant, who asked Peter, "How's the P & L look?"

Peter said, "If P is profit, and L is loss, we're all L".

Still, that first year we made money.

Radio at the time was sold by spots, or commercial packages called "flights." We started doing special packages. Offutt Air Force base was there and we did something called the "Offutt News." We got a $3,000 a month loan from a bank. That was some kind of a contract in 1965. We also sponsored special events and started going into the black. The station was beginning to get some notice and it was returning money so Buckley said, "Well, it seems to me we could do more of these. Let's form a company."

The Sting

In May of 1966, we founded Starr Broadcasting Group, Incorporated (SBGI). The idea was we would buy and manage radio stations. But here was the deal: Bill owned 66.67% of the company because, as he said, "I've got the name and I've got the money." It made a lot of sense at the time. Peter and I owned the last third of the company and Peter had a majority of *that*. He and I were supposed to go out and audition the stations, then buy and operate them successfully. If we did an event in a town, Bill would come to it as publicity for the radio station. The biggest thing was that Bill was supposed to provide the money. Didn't happen.

The first station we managed was KOWH because Buckley already owned it. The new company didn't have any money so KOWH stayed under Buckley's ownership until we made our first public offering three years later. When Buckley bought KOWH-AM in 1957, it was connected to an FM station called KQAL at 94.1 FM. However, KQAL was not on the air because Todd Storz had taken it "silent" in 1949 in order to concentrate on KOWH. In 1960, Buckley put it back on the air as KMEO at 91.4 FM. In 1968 we changed the call letters to KOWH-FM and changed the genre to album-oriented rock (AOR). In the mid-1960s, the AM was re-named "KOZN 55 Dozen, Your Country Cuzin." The slogan was a multiplication problem: 55 x 12 = 660, our place on the AM dial.

In 1971, KOWH-FM became known informally as "Radio Free Omaha" until we sold both the AM and FM stations to an African American company headed by St. Louis Cardinals pitcher (and Omaha hometown hero) Bob Gibson. In his book, *Stranger to the Game* (1994) Gibson wrote, "I don't think I understood the full meaning of the word bigotry until I tried to sell advertising time for KOWH. Almost none of the established businesses would buy from us and they searched hard for reasons not to."

The Air Force and Me

I wasn't drafted but I was about to be. When I learned from my mother in 1966 that I had mail from the draft board in Stamford,

Connecticut, I walked across the street from Georgetown Law to a recruiting office for the Air Force and basically asked, "Whaddya got?"

They had appointments for Judge Advocate General's (JAG) officers and I had to be in Texas in two days. I was engaged to be married in October of 1967, and when I told my pending wife, Ellen, about it, she was very upset. I asked Bill Buckley to get in touch with the two Nebraska senators. I had already volunteered for Vietnam so it wasn't like I was trying to get out of it—I just wanted to get married before I went.

In early 1966 I graduated from Georgetown and drove to Texas for basic training, which included combat training in case we were assigned to Vietnam, which I knew I was. We trained together with the chaplains. We were such poor marchers they took us off the parade field at Lackland Air Force Base and we marched in the parking lot of the chapel. I didn't know an enlisted man from a general. I saluted everybody. But I survived.

However, while there I received a letter saying that my assignment to Vietnam had been cancelled and I would be posted somewhere in Southeast Asia instead. I never was. I guessed Buckley and the two Nebraska senators came through.

I reported for duty at Strategic Air Command (SAC) Headquarters at Offutt Air Force Base near Bellevue, Nebraska and was assigned to the JAG office of the 3902nd Air Base Wing. I had *hated* law school. Nevertheless, for the next three years I was a lawyer in the JAG office, discovering that I liked trial work and I was good at it.

I had met Ellen Marie Savage when I was at Georgetown Law and she was at Trinity College at Catholic University. Ellen had Juvenile Diabetes, a very bad case of it, and she eventually lost her sight. She just was not able to manage her life very well, and I can't say that I contributed because I was not there as much as I should have been. In those early years, I was preoccupied with the Air Force and the business, and even after I left the Air Force, there was always the business.

Our baby, Colleen, was born with diabetes and died within the first week. I believe Ellen thought that I blamed her because of her diabetes, but I did not. Ellen and I later adopted two children, Sian and Michael, Jr.

After we married in 1967, things got a little stressful between Peter and Ellen. She felt that Peter monopolized my time and got upset that he assumed he had Carte Blanche to come to dinner every night. He would call each night to ask what was on the menu. Things got a little dicey as time went on but, on the whole, relations between Peter and me were good between 1967 and 1977. (Ellen passed in 1996.)

The Air Force had an exercise called Broken Arrow to train for when a plane is going down or has gone down. One time in Omaha, I had just driven out of the base gates and a C-135 was taking off at the same time. I noticed that the plane was settling in as it flew over the roadway, not gaining altitude, and immediately afterwards the plane crashed. I had all this training for the Broken Arrow and I happened to be the first one there. I parked, ran down the hillside, but the plane erupted with thirteen huge explosions, even singeing my uniform. Everybody, save one man who hadn't been strapped in, got out of the plane alive.

I had been on my way to a meeting at the bank about Starr Broadcasting, and when I walked into the bank office later, everybody saw my singed uniform and wanted to know what had happened. So, I had to explain what a hero I had been.

A Day at the Library

When Todd Storz owned KOWH, he boosted the station to number one among independents in America partly by his Top Forty music and his crazy on-air promotions. We felt promotions helped Starr bring in the listeners again.

At the time we went to work for Buckley, the station was not doing well and was listed with an asterisk in the ratings book. That meant we had "no measurable audience." One of our earliest promotions to turn that around was also one of our best. Inspired by Todd Storz, we held what was called a "treasure hunt," whereby the station announced that a $1,000 bill had been placed in a book somewhere in the Omaha Public Library.

I got a call from the panicked library manager: "They're tearing the library apart!" Once it was all over, the library sent me a bill for $40,000, but the damage just proved that the ratings were wrong, we *did* have a "measurable audience."

The KOWH purchase price included an airplane the station owned. It had a traveling message sign on the wings, which a lot of people had at the time, but not like we did; it was beautifully lit up. We used to make a bundle flying over the University of Nebraska football games. One day, the pilot did what he was supposed to do, flew around the field on the first pass and ran the messages, but then he was gone. He stole the plane. To me it was unbelievable. Sometime in the 1970s I got a call from Arizona. They had my plane. After all those years. It had apparently been used for business in Phoenix. Somebody traced the number on the engine block and found out we owned it and we got the plane back.

Buford and the Bank

It's important to understand that I was working in three major directions at once during those days. While in the Air Force, Ellen and I were also newlyweds. Simultaneously, I was working with Peter as much as I could at KOWH and Starr Broadcasting, trying to come up with working capital as well as radio stations. As a matter of fact, when we formed Starr Broadcasting, we did so in the Air Force Liason Office in Omaha, where I had been assigned after doing some brief legal work. The liason office was in my house.

We were operating stations and acquiring stations. It was a great arrangement. (As you will learn, we had eleven radio stations by 1971.) Things were different and more complex at the FCC until Jimmy Carter became president and began deregulation. Even so, we were building a corporate culture.

Until I married in October 1967, Peter and I shared an apartment. We had a wonderful time together, and it was first time we had been under one roof for an extended period since August 1960.

I was finishing my tour in the Air Force at Offutt Air Force Base, located near the big Omaha stockyards. The bank was located in the middle of all these cattle wandering around in different pens. Nobody else in town would even talk to me about a loan, so I went to the Stockyards National Bank. I had to walk through the cattle to get to the front door.

There was a banker there from Wichita and we really hit it off. He said, "I want to come out and see your business." We had a tower and building on forty acres of land. None of it was encumbered by debt. He came out and said yes, he would lend us the fifty thousand dollars, but he said, "I'm going to have to have your father co-sign the note."

"Oh," I said, "that's good. It so happens he's in the car today." He wasn't, of course. I said, "Give me the note, I'll go have him sign it and I'll bring it back in."

I walked out, signed it myself, and when I brought it back, Peter and I had fifty thousand dollars to use for working capital. But I also had to buy some cattle because it was the Stockyards National Bank. We selected a couple of animals—including "Buford the Bull"—and we had them grazing on our forty acres.

Later, the owner of several supermarkets wanted to buy commercial time for his businesses. He had twenty-eight stores and I said, "We'll take a corral around to some of your locations and put a steer or bull in the corral and listeners can come out and guess the weight. The person who guesses the weight of the animal wins it."

We were out at the first location in Omaha, with a huge crowd around our wooden corral, and Buford the Bull was in the ring. Buford was blindfolded because we didn't want him to be spooked by the crowd, but somehow the blindfold came off. Buford dug his front paws into the ground and headed straight for the corral fence. He broke through and ran over the owner of the supermarket chain. Buford ran down the street and I had to call the police to go get him because, of course, the winner wanted the bull. I visited the owner of the supermarkets in the hospital and he said, "You know, I'm a little beat up," (he was a whole lot beat up) "but that's the best promotion I've ever seen anybody do!"

The Damage Store was the sponsor for another KOWH promotion. We did a twenty-eight car giveaway for the store, owned by

Leo Kraft. We went to a used car dealer and he agreed to take some advertising and, as part of the deal, he had to give us a car a day to give away on the air during the month of February. As we were about to start the promotion, we went over to look at the cars one more time but there weren't any on the lot. They had been repossessed. We didn't have the twenty-eight cars we needed. We had to go out and buy junk cars every day.

Part of the promotion involved going to the Damage Store every day to see if your key opened the treasure chest. If so, you got the winning "quality pre-owned car" that day. The sponsor called up the first day and said "Get these people out of here. They're ruining my store." I said, "You're a damage store, how could they ruin it?"

We were so pressed every day to come up with a car that we didn't do a whole lot of inspecting. Once, we were at the bottom of a hill on this acreage we owned, and one of these cars came cascading down the driveway and ran into the side of the building because the brakes didn't work. Another day—I, personally, was there for this one—a proud winner and her mother-in-law and their husbands got in the car. The mother-in-law stepped on the flood board and immediately her shoes went through. She slipped about halfway down to the street. We wound up buying replacement cars to replace the replacement cars.

As we had figured, by not selling individual commercials, or spots, and instead selling events and packages we made tons of money and nobody could figure out how we were doing it.

Liar Liar

There came a time when the wool was off everybody's eyes, and we finally knew Buckley really didn't have any money.

The same banker who had been at the Stockyards Bank in Omaha and lent me the money for Buford (among other things), became vice president of a bank in Kansas City called the Columbia Union National Bank. The loan officer there was Glenn Burris, and the president of the bank was a guy named Robert Wallerstedt.

When Peter or Buckley had personal investments they wanted to make, I was usually the one that arranged the money. Buckley wanted a fifty thousand dollar personal loan from Columbia Union National Bank. I wondered, why did he have me go to Kansas City to get him fifty thousand dollars? Why couldn't he just pick up the phone to his New York banker and get it? That was kind of suspicious in the first place, but I said, "I will get it for you," and I did. My penance for doing that was I had to agree to have a meeting with Ed McMahon (of *Tonight Show* fame), and help him get a movie produced. It was a liquid lunch, I'll say that much. But Buckley signed the note for fifty thousand dollars, I kept the McMahon meeting, Buckley got the money, and then he didn't pay it back.

Buckley denied he signed the note. *He said it was forged.* Now I was the guy who's on the hook for the money.

Wallerstedt called Bill about the overdue loan and, again, Bill said, "The note's a forgery."

Wallerstedt said, "Okay, we're all coming to New York and we're going to meet in your multimillion dollar condo at 778 Park Ave," which was a Taj Mahal. We all went to see Bill in New York and Wallerstedt said, "Okay Bill, tell me again."

Bill said, "Uh...uh...well...the note's forged."

Wallerstedt told Buckley, "Hand me the telephone. What's the number of the FBI?"

"Well, maybe...oh yes," Buckley said. "How did I forget that?"

Buckley finally paid up.

Talk about a really pretentious guy. He had a big limousine, and we would ride in the back of the limo with him as we drove around Manhattan. Most people only had one phone line in their limousine, but he had two. If he was on the phone, the chauffeur would answer the other one and say, "I'm sorry, Mr. Buckley's on the other line."

I mean...in a car?

Chapter 5

Good Morning Starrshine

The Best Little City in America

In 1966, the FCC approved our first acquisition under the Starr Broadcasting Group label. We found a full-time radio station in Sioux Falls, South Dakota called KISD-AM, the first rock and roll station in South Dakota. Operating twenty-four hours a day, KISD was situated at Joe Foss Field, named after the famous World War II pilot.

Before Starr got involved, the station was owned by Verl Thomson in Sioux Falls and he broadcast out of the basement of his house on 1230 AM, 1,000 watts. There really was not much in between the small towns in South Dakota, so even if you had a big fifty thousand watt blowtorch, it wouldn't have mattered.

So, here we go...and it's our *first* acquisition.

"Okay, Bill, it costs two hundred thousand to buy this."

"Wellllll," says Bill Buckley, "I don't have twenty thousand dollars handy, but I'll give you fifty thousand for a down payment."

We went back to the owner and said, "We're novices. We've got fifty thousand dollars, and we'll give you paper for the rest of it." We actually did a deal for fifty down, mainly because we didn't have two hundred thousand, even though Buckley said he'd get it for us. We convinced Verl Thomson to take four hundred dollars a week for the radio station until it was paid off. Years later, Verl's daughter Ginger became Miss South Dakota.

That's the first fifty thousand dollars we ever invested. At the end of the game, when we stopped acquiring in the mid-1970s, Buckley's total investment in *the whole company* was one hundred fifty thousand dollars. At even new acquisition opportunity, we had to figure how we were going to buy it, finance it, operate it, and sell it. Yes, he put up that first fifty thousand, but he was supposed to put up all the money for all the purchases and this first deal didn't bode very well for what the future was going to be like. I was always saying to myself, "Ok...what am I gonna pull to solve *this* problem?"

We started operations by hiring an air staff from Arizona that we flew in the night before we went on the air. The station was an immediate hit, and we sold it a few years later for seven hundred thousand dollars. Not only did we perform on what we said we would do, we brought home the bacon and by then we were thinking, "Well, maybe Bill didn't have the money at the time...."

The KISD radio station tower was on our acreage along with the world's only Train Motel. It was called the Sioux Chief Traintel and basically consisted of three Pullman cars and a coach car. On a Tuesday afternoon, some guy with a boom truck, who had been drinking at a bar near the Traintel, was driving down the street, passed out at the wheel, and ran into one of the tower's guide wires. According to the Sioux Falls *Argus Leader*, the station was knocked off the air for more than six hours. Verl Thomson implied that if the tower had fallen west instead of east, the Traintel would have been smashed. Instead, some late sleepers in the Traintel were simply a little surprised. The motel remained in business until 1975, and the cars were moved in May 1990.

At this point in Starr's history, of course, we still have no money, and now we had to replace the tower. In the meantime, we had to get that radio station back on the air. In those days, if a tower went down you took two utility poles and ran a wire between them. That was a way to get some signal on the air, and that's what we did until we finally got insurance money to pay for it.

Bill told the New York newspapers that he bought a station in Sioux Falls (known by its official nickname "The Best Little City in America"), because he was trying to bolster the "economic end" of the *National Review*. "All journals of opinion," he said, "have to own something. *The New Republic* (a journal of Liberal opinion) owns an envelope factory."

Kansas City Starr

Got a letter just this morning, it was postmarked Omaha
It was typed and neatly written
Offering me this better job…
…But I'm on TV here locally
I can't quit, I'm a star…
…I'm the king of Kansas City
No thanks, Omaha, thanks a lot

Kansas City Star,
That's what I arrrrrre…[43]

Two years later, in 1968, we all became "Kansas City Starrs" by acquiring two radio stations from two different owners. The first one was KUDL. We got a call from the biggest media broker in the country at that time, Blackburn & Company. They had listed an AM in Kansas City—KUDL. The interesting thing about this deal is that the station was owned by Gene Burdick, who was the co-author of two famous books, *Fail Safe* and *The Ugly American*. He died in 1965 at the age of forty-six, and we did business with his widow in California. The Blackburn broker was a fascinating fellow by the name of Colin Self. We met him in San Francisco at the Fairmont Hotel, another thing we couldn't pay for in those days. Actually, we weren't altogether sure how we were going to get back to Omaha.

Self said to us, "I'm gonna show you how to buy this radio station." We drank in the bar at the Fairmont from midnight to six in the morning. The meeting with Burdick's widow was set for eight, but by six in the morning we knew exactly what to do. This lady had some younger children and she didn't want any money then, as Colin Self had warned us. She told us she would sell us the station on paper. Nothing down. And no payments until *fourteen years* after the date of the transfer of the license. That was a relief because we were finding out that Buckley couldn't be relied on financially. What's not to do with a deal like that? That's a top 100 market. A fourteen year note, low capital costs, and we didn't have to call Buckley for anything, which wouldn't have mattered because he didn't have it.

Before we got approval from the Federal Communications Commission (FCC) to buy KUDL in March of 1967, the *Kansas City Star* ran a story on the station's recent switch from Top Forty to mostly talk with phone calls and jazz at night. The program director was asked if the sale to Starr and Buckley would affect programming policies on KUDL. The director said, "Buckley, as far as I know, doesn't get embroiled in broadcasting other than on his own television show out of New York... So, it is merely a change in ownership and will not affect our programming concept in any way."

In less than a year, KUDL was back to Top Forty in Kansas City.

Some of you may be asking the question: "Why did you stay with Buckley if he wouldn't give you any money and you had to do all that hard work to build the company without his support?"

Well, we were young. No mature person was going to take an offer like that, but we didn't know any better. We were novices. I suppose that part of it also had to do with our long history with Bill. And maybe Peter and I liked the art of the deal, just like Donald Trump.

But, when things first got dicey financially, we realized, like the lady in the commercial who asked "Where's the beef?" that it was sink or swim. When Peter and I didn't know whether we could close a certain deal or not, we knew we literally might have to get out of town. That's how young we were. We even researched extradition and found that there was no extradition from Brazil for civil matters, at least at that time. Brazil became *our* country. That's where we would go if we had to.

How I Messed Up, and Met Ed McConwell

The second station we acquired in Kansas City in 1967 was KCJC-FM. Ed McConwell represented the owner, his father-in-law Ruben Sell. Appropriately, Ruben wanted to *sell* KCJC and Peter and I wanted to buy it.

Peter and Ed negotiated the original agreement with a fifteen year payout for the station because we were buying everything on a leveraged basis at that point (since we couldn't get any money from Bill anyway). Peter negotiated a long term note and we had certain monthly obligations as well. Somehow in the blur of everything that was going on, we—that is *I*, specifically—missed a payment on the note for the station. Ed came over and, the first time I ever met him, we had to talk about what the solution was going to be.

Ed had negotiated and written into the agreement an acceleration provision (calling for immediate payment of the entire note) and he implemented the acceleration but, thank God, we ultimately renegotiated it down to two or three years.

I was never mad at Ed about it. It was my responsibility. I made the mistake. If they had called in the loan it would have triggered a default on a lot of other loans. So almost any relief that avoided that would have been saving the day. Ed McConwell understood that and he worked out something that was both good for his father-in-law and a salvation to Starr.

I would always remember that day–I knew how bad the penalty could have been and Ed was rational about it, and so was everybody else. It was a tough beginning to a relationship, but it brought us together and Ed McConwell eventually became a jack-of-all-trades. Peter became his primary client. Although he never officially represented me, Ed became a friend of the family when we closed our first public offering in 1969. We all went to Bermuda together, Ed, his wife Linda, Peter, and I. We were all good friends over the years.

Who Is Jeff Christie?

In 1969, KCJC-FM became KUDL-FM, so we had both KUDL (1380-AM) and KUDL (98.1-FM). The AM side played oldies for a while, simulcasting with the FM side, but in 1975, KUDL-AM went all news and talk. This was programmed by a service owned by the NBC network. The AM had just hired a guy who used the name Jeff Christie on the air. His real name was Rush Limbaugh, but nobody knew he was Rush Limbaugh, not even himself. He blames his mother for his winding up at Starr Broadcasting.

One day in June of 2010, Rush recounted on his now famous syndicated radio show that he was sitting—out of work and tanning himself—in the backyard of his home in Missouri when his mother came out of the house and said there was a phone call for him from a guy in Kansas City who was offering him a job. The call had come from our own Jim Carnegie at KUDL. Rush told his mother to take a number. Apparently, his mother said, "No, you are coming in and you are taking the call, and if you are offered a job, you are going."

"And the next day I was in my car on the way to Kansas City."[44]

The general public is not aware that Rush Limbaugh was not always Rush Limbaugh, including my brother Paul, who was working for Starr when Rush joined us in Kansas City. Paul tells it this way:

> I was reading a book about Rush Limbaugh back in the early nineties and I got to the part where he was hired by Starr Broadcasting at KUDL, and I thought *Wait a minute, I should have known him.* I read the chapter and they mentioned that his on air name was "Jeff Christie," and that was the first time I even realized that I had known Rush Limbaugh. Then, about three or four years later, I found some old file folders and in one of them were three memos to me from Jeff Christie, dated about 1975 or '76. They related to public affairs programming and they were signed "Jeff Christie" except for the final one, which I found was signed "Jeff Christie, aka Rush Limbaugh." It was probably that last one in which he was actually kind of humorous. I had wondered why they had not aired any public affairs programs in the week prior—that's the kind of thing I checked on—and he was responding to me about this great interview he had done with some city official in Kansas City. It might have been the mayor, but it did not air because the station, at the last minute, decided to carry a hockey game. He really let his frustration show in the memo.
>
> That is my recollection of Rush Limbaugh. I used to go to all the stations, I knew just about everybody around the group. I can't even pull up a picture in my mind of Jeff Christie/Rush Limbaugh.

In a rather interesting bit of irony, our station decided that Rush would not be a good fit on the talk side, so he was moved over to KUDL-FM. He found a way to talk anyway, then found a listenership. However, in his 2010 book on Limbaugh, author Zev Chafets notes that Limbaugh was fired from KUDL in 1978, which was not unusual, because Limbaugh "had personality conflicts with superiors who found him argumentative."[45]

After KUDL, Limbaugh wound up working for the Kansas City Royals for five years, where George Brett had befriended him. In 1983, he landed at KMBZ in Kansas City and apparently started using his real name there. The next year, Morton Downey Junior was fired at KFBK in Sacramento and Rush auditioned for his job. [46]

Rush parlayed his show into a vehicle that turned him into one of America's hot new Talk Show Conservatives. He appeared on Buckley's *Firing Line* more than once. Another connection between Rush Limbaugh and Buckley came to light years later. In *The American Conservative*, John Derbyshire wrote:

> Limbaugh has a similarly high opinion of himself: "I know I have become the intellectual engine of the conservative movement," he told the New York Times...Upon discovering that Limbaugh had anointed himself the successor to William F. Buckley Jr., WFB's son Christopher retorted, "Rush, I knew William F. Buckley, Jr. William F. Buckley, Jr. was a father of mine. Rush, you're no William F. Buckley, Jr."[47]

In 1975 we changed the call letters from KUDL to KCNW and the format became all news. We sold KCNW three years later to Universal Broadcasting and they put in place a religious format.

Chapter 6

Everything's OK

The OK Stations—We "Go Public"

The Starr Broadcasting Group, Inc., of Omaha has purchased three out-of-state radio stations Peter H. Starr, president, announced Friday. Starr declined to give the purchase price.... The stations are WBOK, New Orleans, La., KYOK, Houston, Tex., and WLOK, Memphis, Tenn.[48]

Three Million Dollars. Ok, Pony Up, Bill.

"Wellll...how much is the escrow?" Bill Buckley wanted to know.

We answered, "One hundred thousand dollars."

Buckley said, "Alright, I'll get you the one hundred thousand. We'll put up the escrow, and we have to pay three hundred thousand back to the person I got this one hundred thousand from for the escrow. And you lads have got to go out and find 2.9 million dollars somewhere."

We did. We were the youngest entrepreneurs in an Initial Public Offering (IPO) in history. I was 27 and Peter was 26. Unbelievable. We got a string of investment banks to put together a syndicate, and they bought an offering of more than $3.5 million. But we were able then to pay for the OK stations.

We went to an investment banker in Omaha called First Investment Securities and they underwrote it. Investment banks all over the country subscribed to this deal. It was over-subscribed. We concocted the "Starr Trek Tour," where we traveled around the country and spoke to analysts at breakfasts and luncheons to hype the stock. We rented a Lear jet we didn't have the money for and flew to the cities.

We really researched it, and then filed to go "public." In addition to WLOK, WBOK, and KYOK (the "OK" stations), the package also included KXLR in North Little Rock, Arkansas.

After filing with the FCC to purchase the stations, we filed with the Securities and Exchange Commission to offer a total of three and a half to four million dollars in stock to the public.[49]

The OK stations were controversial because they were all black programming and on-air personnel. In those days the FCC license approval called them "negro-oriented formats." They were owned by Stanley Ray and Jules Paglin of New Orleans. All three were big profit makers. The sellers did not want to have their financials put in our Securities and Exchange Commission offering because they figured, when their listeners found out how much they were making off those radio stations, there was going to be trouble. It turns out that we were just on the borderline of when trouble really began.

Stanley Ray was a shrewd guy who, on the beaches of Angio, sent an application for the license for WBOK 1230 AM in New Orleans, and by the time he got back from the war it had been awarded. Paglin put up the money. It was an amazing success for them, as was WLOK in Memphis and KYOK in Houston.

The sale to Starr was approved by a 5-to-2 vote in May of 1969: Robert Bartley and Nicholas Johnson dissented.[50] It's my recollection that this was actually the second vote on the licenses, the first being a 4-to-3 vote *against* the sale, and that Starr petitioned for a re-hearing and was granted one, which resulted in the ultimate 5-to-2 vote in favor of Starr Broadcasting. It's also possible that the 4-to-3 vote was an "in house" straw vote. At any rate, the FCC gave its approval.

May of 1969 was a good month for me. It was also the month I was discharged from the Air Force.

Before 1969 we were a privately held company. Our public offering put us on the Midwest Stock Exchange, which doesn't exist anymore. We also tried to get on the American Stock Exchange but that exchange required a certain level of *tangible* assets and in broadcasting you don't have many tangible assets for the size of the profit they generate. I went to see them every year but they wouldn't write us up.

The purchase of the three OK stations and 'going public' by being listed on the Midwest Stock Exchange was a big step for the Starr brand. Our first *Annual Report* was published on June 30, 1969. The eventual value of the Starr stations that Peter and I built was absolutely unbelievable: hundreds of millions of dollars.

MLK, the Rabbit, and Me

In 1968, after we bought the OK stations but before we had official FCC approval in 1969, we were doing kind of a Lease Management Agreement (LMA). We had not closed with the FCC, but we were spending time in each one of the stations doing "due diligence," which allowed us to satisfy ourselves about the honesty of the operations and also to be on site for the sake of our employees.

WLOK in Memphis was an urban station, as was WBOK in New Orleans and KYOK in Houston. On April 4, Martin Luther King was assassinated at the Lorraine Motel in Memphis not far from WLOK. The town went nuts. Tensions in Memphis had been exacerbated recently by growing resentment, "especially at stations with all black programming that claimed to be the 'voice' of the black community, but were white-owned and controlled by white management."[51]

The mostly African-American staff told me that they had to get me out of there, which I was pleased to hear. But the only thing they had to hide me to get me out of the building was the mascot uniform for the radio station, a fairly large rabbit. So, the employees stuffed me into the rabbit suit, and then I got stuffed into the back of a car and driven out of the area to the Holiday Inn Rivermont in downtown Memphis. I was still a rabbit, and checked in as a rabbit. I undressed in my room. It was quite an affair.

I never made very much about it because I was not for publicity in those days, and it was such a sensitive thing I could see the headlines: "White owner of black station escapes as the Easter Bunny."

I had friends at that same time who owned black stations in other parts of the country and a number of them had to deal with mobs. Some of their stations were even burned down. Starr didn't have any of that, but if the people in the street that day had any idea I was there, I think it would have been a bad scene.

Starr Broadcasting: How We Sound—1969

A short audio presentation was included as a vinyl disc in the first annual report to let the original shareholders know more about their new company and it's first small group of stations. You can listen to this ten minute bit of history by going online to YouTube and entering "Starr Broadcasting How We Sound Annual Report 1969."

Labor Pains

While Starr obviously was not the first white ownership of these stations, we did run into some labor problems.

> Late in 1970, on-air staff walked out of WLOK protesting low wages and poor working conditions. After a 10-day strike and a series of negotiations that lasted several months…WLOK hired the first African-American station manager, Harvey E. Lynch. Further-more, white ownership came to understand that the all-black programming staff knew more about what their listening audience wanted from a station…[52]

My brother John was affected by labor unrest at our New Orleans station, WBOK:

> I decided I wanted to get in the radio business but I didn't want to come in as the brother who didn't know anything about radio, either. So, I got a job at a radio station in Charleston, SC as an announcer. I was doing overnights while I was in the Air Force, learning the radio business, and upon my honorable discharge in January of 1972, I went to New Orleans and joined Starr Broadcasting at WBOK. I was an account executive, not on the air.

At WBOK there was a strike by the announcers, and management came to me and said, "Weren't you an announcer in Charleston?"

I said, "Yes, but it was a country station."

They said they needed an announcer because all of the announcers were on the street. So I became a disc jockey at WBOK, a black music station. I went on the air and they told me "don't talk, just segue," meaning no announcing in between records. I did that for eight hours a day. There were three of us and we each had an eight hour shift. The strike lasted about a week. The strike was about the lack of black management and it was settled when one of the disc jockeys was made program director. The FCC was paying attention to white ownership of black radio stations.

We did a lot of what was called "ascertainment." I remember doing some ascertainment at one time and my brother Paul did too. Paul said to me, "John, I've got a problem. I did a music ascertainment with the general public, and I interviewed mainly blacks. One of the questions was 'what type of music should be played on WBOK?' He said that fifty-seven percent answered 'Classics.'"

My brother Paul's degree is in classic languages, and he said, "Classics? How can that be?" He thought they meant classical music.

So, I said to my brother, "Did you ask them what kind?"

He said, "No."

I told him, "Ask them what kind of classics they mean." So he went back and re-did the survey and did as I'd suggested.

The answer came back, "You know, like James Brown."

Snakes in Arkansas

You may know that Arkansas is famous for snakes. At the same time the FCC approved our purchase of the OK stations, they also approved our purchase of KXLR-AM, a country and western station in Little Rock.

The previous owner, Frank Lynch, was a character who always walked around with a Bible. We were holding a farewell party for Frank and his family after we purchased the station. He drank quite a bit and at the end of the party he finally got up and said, "I want to go around the table and thank each one of my employees who did so much for the station. Over here we have Joe Francis. Joe, maybe you didn't know that I knew, but I knew you were stealing toilet paper out of the station." He just laid them out for various offenses and never said a nice word about anybody. I never saw anything like it.

The station had six towers and four of them went out into a swamp filled with water moccasins. We acquired fifty-five drums of oil that we poured all over the place because, theoretically, the snakes would not go through it. That proved to be not entirely correct. In the control room of that station there were big guns because occasionally a snake would get into the building. Nobody, of course, would go out to the swamp and read the meters.

One day the FCC showed up and cited us for not taking the meter readings. I gave them a clipboard for tower number one and said "You go take the readings." The guy came back ashen-faced. A water moccasin was sunning itself on one of the tower doors and when he opened the door, the snake came with it and landed right at the guy's feet. He said, "You don't *never* have to take another reading again."

At WLOK in Memphis, we found that paid commercials were being logged, or recorded, as Public Service Announcements, which were no charge, so the owners were not reporting the money. There were two white managers, and the black employees had turned them in. We finally realized during our "due diligence" that we should take the logs for one day and see if the recordings for that day matched the log. The employees were right. I made a presentation to the station managers at the Holiday Inn in Memphis and, without saying a word in their defense, they just handed me their keys.

It turned out that Stanley Ray, who had sold those stations to us, had paid every manager a bonus. But when he found out they had been stealing from him all those years, he demanded the bonuses back. It was really ugly stuff. What a novel way to steal. I never would have thought of it.

Chapter 7

1970—Off and Running

Religion in Big D and TV in Tennessee

In 1970 we got religion by getting religion. We had begun to figure out that AM radio was going to all be eliminated by FM, and over the next few years we made an effort to buy every FM we could get our hands on. We discovered KEIR, a 100 thousand watt FM station in Dallas. A preacher, William Robert Elkins, better known as "Billy Bob" Elkins owned it. I'll never forget the first time I went into his office and saw that it was all fur—fur floor, fur walls, fur everything. All white fur.

We took this station, quickly changed the call letters to KDTX-FM, and made it one of the first twenty-four hour religion stations in the country. We sold the sponsor contracts once a year as opposed to selling "flights" of individual spots for 60 or 90 days. What's not to like about that?

Also in 1970, Starr Broadcasting got into TV. We added a beautiful NBC affiliate in the tri-cities: WCYB-TV-5, Bristol, Tennessee; Johnson City, Tennessee; and Bristol, Virginia. We paid five million for it and we were taking a million dollars a year in cash out of it. Once again—no Buckley. By now we had a pretty good reputation and the company was doing so well that I was able to go to the banks and get the kind of deals I wanted. I got one hundred percent financing on that television station because the station was doing so well.

The Chemical Bank in New York gave us a letter of credit for five hundred thousand dollars, and I got that with no signatures or anything, just the guarantee of the company. That was a tremendous buy.

The station was tops in the ratings partly because of two men: Walter Crockett did the station editorials for many years and news anchor Merrill Moore was the big gun in news from the time he joined the station in 1962 until he retired in 2000.

Overseas Stockholders

FCC rules allowed foreign ownership to the extent of twenty-five percent of the outstanding control stock of a broadcast company. The Skye Trust in Scotland made a big investment in the company, as did the Hong Kong and Shanghai Banking Corporation (HSBC). Once a year we went to Edinburgh, Scotland and to Hong Kong to have a stockholders meeting. It was a 'round-the-world trip, which I really miss a lot.

Fourth Time's Not the Charm: Trying to Buy WCAM-AM

Continuing with our record year, in 1970, we also added WCAM-AM, licensed to the city of Camden, New Jersey and serving Philadelphia. It was actually owned by the city of Camden. The mayor, Joe Nardi, explained that the city was in financial crisis so we agreed to *pre-pay* him for the station. I borrowed the money from Chemical Bank before we closed on the sale. We were the fourth group to try to buy the station:

> After three unsuccessful attempts in four years to sell WCAM (AM) Camden, N.J., the city of Camden last week found another prospective buyer in Starr Broadcasting Groups Inc. The New Orleans based group owner will buy the station for $1.45 million, subject to the signing of a formal agreement and FCC approval.[53]

We wound up batting clean-up in this mess because, five years earlier, the city of Camden had turned down a 1.35 million dollar offer because the prospective buyers were financially shaky. Then, later in the year, the FCC rejected the sale of the station to Gordon McLendon for the same amount. In 1966, the FCC called for a hearing because it was concerned whether the programming plans of proposed owners Phil and Leonard Chess, founders of Chess Records, "were designed for the large Negro audience of Philadelphia."[54] I guess the commissioners had never heard of Muddy Waters, Bo Diddley, Etta James, or Chuck Berry.

Next, it was our turn at bat. One of the parties who was interviewed by the FCC during the ascertainment process was an elderly Catholic priest. He didn't remember the interview at all, and said he was never interviewed. For this and other reasons, a station community group was able to block the completion of the sale. We saw at that point that it was going to be an FM world anyway, so all we wanted was our (prepaid) money back.

Peter and I happened to be walking down the street in New Orleans, and we ran into none other than Camden mayor Joe Nardi. He was in town for a convention.

I yelled at him, "Joe, I want my money." Of course, it attracted a whole lot of attention.

Nardi answered, "I don't have it."

We said, "Look, Mr. Mayor, you can do whatever you wanna do. You can have the station back, you can do whatever you want to do, but our company's gonna get liquidated if you don't give us that money back."

Starr Broadcasting kept WCAM-AM listed in our annual report for two years as a "*pending acquisition.*" That's how long this thing dragged out. We never got WCAM-AM, though we did finally get our money back.

The Coral Gables Disaster

In 1973, we put up a building in Coral Gables for SITCO, our company that owned outdoor theaters and would later figure in the downfall of Starr Broadcasting. As the building project progressed, we discovered a major construction error that caused the Hotel

Ponce de Leon next door to slide into the hole where our office building was supposed to be. It was on TV all over the country. The
excavation was not done properly, the lateral support for the hotel
disappeared, and it became a waterborne hotel—in the water of our
excavation. We had sunk steel pilings and they were supposed to keep
the water out, but didn't. The water got into the excavation and the
hotel went into the hole. We finished the building, but by that time
SITCO was in such a mess we decided to sell it. Somehow we did. It
was a beautiful building but we should have seen it for the bad omen
it was.

The Kenner Office Building

We moved Starr headquarters from Omaha to New Orleans in 1970,
settling in the First National Life building at 1000 Howard Avenue.
Three years later, we constructed a new building of our own in the
New Orleans bedroom community of Kenner, Louisiana. It was built
by the same contractor who built the nightmare in Florida. Same
guy. Now you should know that the only reason we used this guy for
both projects is that they were started *simultaneously*. He did manage
to finish this project at 3715 Williams Boulevard pretty well and we
were based out of that building from 1973 to 1977. I noticed about
twenty years later that the thing was falling apart. Recently it has been
rehabbed and now the building looks pretty good again.

Synergizing Starr Broadcasting

In the early '70s we started what is called today "diversifying." This
was encouraged to create a "synergy" within the business, a balance,
where one category of investments or projects benefits the others, even
though they are in different categories.

In 1970, we bought Arlington House publishing, which also
owned a conservative book club, a nostalgia book club, and a nostalgia
record club. That thing made money. Neil McCaffrey sold us the
company. He was a friend of Bill Buckley's, and the lead on this publishing company that was the one solid thing we ever got out of Bill

besides money, of which we got very little. That year's annual report summarized the company, saying,

> Arlington House is a New Rochelle based publisher that has gained a significant reputation particularly in the areas of politics and economics. Among the company's books this year were the influential *The Emerging Republican Majority*, by Kevin Phillips and *How You Can Profit from the Coming Devaluation*, by Harry Browne…
>
> The company's two book clubs, The Conservative Book Club, and The Nostalgia Book club, have a total membership of about 40,000.[55]

When Israel was founded in 1948, a huge issue dedicated to the state of Israel was published by *Time*. In 1973, on its 25th anniversary, the state of Israel came up with a beautiful commemoration book including the *Time* issue from 1948, which is really a collector's item. Arlington House had the U.S. rights to it. So we printed and sold the book to synagogues all over the country. I've still got a couple of copies. I am more proud of that than just about anything we ever did in the publishing business.

In 1971, we bought Alan Torbet Associates, a company that represented local radio stations in selling radio commercials (spots) to national sponsors. It allowed stations to sell to a wider market than just local businesses. At the time of purchase by Starr, ATA represented more than one hundred stations around the country and was one of the biggest "radio reps" in the US. Just another example of our aggressive synergy program.

Le-Bo Products—1972

Leslie Bocor and Leslie Dame were born in Hungary. After Hitler and Auschwitz, they returned to Budapest but, in 1956, suffered under the Hungarian Revolution. I was in high school and I was listening to news reports about the revolution on my short wave radio.

All of a sudden, in 1972 I ended up in business with these two Holocaust survivors who had come out of Budapest and in 1958 started a thriving company in Queens, NY. They provided things like carrying cases for tapes and all kinds of accessories for the products developed for the broadcast industry. Le-Bo was enormously success-ful in spite of two facts about the starting of Le-Bo. One, the guys knew only a few words of English in 1958, and two, they originally only sold record racks in two sizes.

They made products that today would have carried CDs, but this was all for the tape industry. They had one model called the 4 Starr, named after us. Just a short list of their products shows how important they were to the broadcasting and music industries: phonograph nee-dles, brushes, adapters, spindles, earphones, loaded blank cassettes, loaded blank tape cartridges, phonograph record racks, carrying cases for phonograph records, reel to reel magnetic tapes, tape cartridges, and tape cassettes.

We got to know Becor and Dame pretty well. We even went to their daughters' weddings, which were very traditional and quite the experiences for Peter and me.

It so happened that in 1972 we were looking for more investment money, so we launched another IPO, but without the "I" because it wasn't "Initial." Still, this stock offering looked much like the one in 1969. Le-Bo had all kinds of earnings. The question was: in that stock offering, could you value stock from a *manufacturing* firm as highly as stock in a *broadcasting* firm? Broadcast had high quality earn-ings. It was a gamble but we did it and "sold out" an offering of 25 and 3/4 per share. This was our second offering and Peter and I were worth a lot of money.

Le-Bo was included in the 1979 transaction when Buckley sold Starr Broadcasting to the Shamrock Corporation, owned by a nephew of Walt Disney. Shamrock "spun off" companies in the package that they did not want to keep. So, they bought Starr Broadcasting, sold off the synergized assets, and didn't pay much for the company at all. In my opinion that sale was a Buckley Blunder—big time.

At the time we bought Le-Bo, however, there was no Buckley involvement. No money, no nothing.

TM Productions: Enter Jim Long

In the broadcast industry, if anyone needed anything innovative in program development by third parties—music libraries, jingles, etc.— TM Productions came to mind first.

TM needed some equipment and the co-founder Jim Long needed some capital, so Peter and I bought the company on October 5, 1971. This is where Buckley's involvement, or lack thereof, really gets interesting.

We didn't have the cash to buy Long's company, and we couldn't borrow it because TM was viewed by the banks to be a speculative business, a little too new and different. It had very few tangible assets and nobody knew at the time what a big deal it was going to be, but it was. It was a home run. We made a deal with TM whereby we would give them a certain amount of cash and a certain amount of stock every year based on profits. Now, if Buckley had been up to his game on what he promised us he would do, we wouldn't have had to do that deal that way. The reason it became important is that Long and his partner were able to add tremendous amounts of stock in their own name as a result of the deal we made to acquire the company.

Jim Long:

> Tom Merriman and I founded TM Productions in 1967 as a jingle company that also programmed beautiful music radio stations. We started out with eleven thousand dollars and that's all the financing we ever had, but we did very well financially and were a profitable company. A broker named Ted Hepburn out of Cincinnati inquired to see if we might be interested in selling the company to someone who would give us expansion money. So, although we were doing well sales-wise and were profitable, we really needed some serious money to expand and to move to a new facility that would house our growing staff. Hepburn brought Peter and Michael Starr to the table. They were very enthusiastic and by that time in 1971, they had gone public with the Midwest Stock Exchange and were making acquisitions.
>
> The Starrs saw the potential in TM and made a deal with us for 1.1 million dollars in cash, plus we would receive a bonus in

Starr stock for our yearly performance above a certain threshold of profitability. It ended up, though, that Starr Broadcasting never put a dime into TM. We expanded from our own internal cash flow, and our deal was structured so that we got to keep the cash profits on hand and we built up a lot of revenue.

The company exploded into new areas, including the creation of IDs that sounded like the hit songs the stations were playing. This was unique in the business, until everybody else started copying us. The company did very well but the interest rates in the early '70s really hammered away at Starr Broadcasting's stock. They dropped from a high of twenty-four dollars a share and each year it went lower, so we got more and more stock. Plus, our profits went up. Tom and I ended up, along with our employees, owning about twenty-six percent of the company, which meant that *together* Tom Merriman and I were a larger shareholder than Bill Buckley.

Starr was very good to me and paid me well. I think I was making about a half a million dollars a year, which was some real money in those days.

TM, based in Dallas, Texas, was positioned to be a big company in the world because we bought it, equipped it, backed it, and TM got the benefit of a price that was adjusted upward every year based on its increased profitability. That's called "dilution." More shares are issued and the people who had a lot of shares (us) have fewer shares. That was bad for Starr and good for TM.

Peter and I had built Starr out of nothing. We bought properties like TM Productions. We built them up well. We made them valuable. And Bill screwed us over. I'm convinced that his betrayal eventually killed my brother. Peter never got over it.

Chapter 8

The Battle of San Francisco

Now, an editorial by Gordon McLendon, president of KABL:

> Tonight at midnight an era ends in Bay Area radio. And, immediately at midnight, a new era begins that we believe will be as dazzling as the morning sun.
>
> Tonight at midnight, after more than thirteen years, the McLendon Corporation hands its ownership of KABL-AM and FM into the hands of the Starr Broadcasting Group, Inc. Starr is wonderfully well managed by two brilliant young brothers, Peter and Mike Starr, who have come up through the ranks as professional broadcasters. They have long loved the Bay Area, and long wanted to own KABL. At midnight tonight they will have it, and God speed...
>
> But go we must, and do, and in doing so leave you with a shining Starr.

The Preceding was editorial comment by Gordon McLendon, President of KABL.[56]

In 1971, we had made a deal to buy KABL-AM and FM in San Francisco for ten million dollars, about the most ever paid for a radio station. KABL had been put on the air as a "beautiful music" station and was a huge success. In fact, our first ratings book inspired us to take out the following ad in the trade papers (which gave an indication of just how unimportant FM was at the time):

DON'T JUST BUY SAN FRANCISCO, OWN IT!
More Bay Area adults 18-49 listen to KABL than to any other station... even if we don't count those who listen to KABL-FM! But
advertisers get both KABL AM and FM in one easy buy.[57]

Extortion by the Bay

A bit of history is necessary to understand what we were up against
in California. As Ronald Garey pointed out in his biography of
Gordon McLendon, KABL-AM used to give a station ID as follows:
"This is Cable, K-A-B-L Oakland, 960 on your dial, in the air,
everywhere—in San Francisco."

Garey said that what most listeners did not know was that "KABL
had not been licensed to serve San Francisco at all. The station
had been assigned to serve Oakland, San Francisco's neighbor across
the bay."

Eventually Oakland city officials complained and the case wound
up before an FCC hearing examiner, who fined McClendon ten thousand dollars. McLendon appealed and the full commission overturned
the fine, saying the wording of the station identification was legal and
proper.[58]

In those days, people roamed the countryside looking for ways to
take down the deals that people were filing with the Federal Communications Commission, unless some goodies went to the
community groups that were striking—opposing—the applications.
So, when we filed for the $10.8 million deal in San Francisco, these
hawks flocked to our doorstep like you wouldn't believe.

I was in San Francisco; Peter was not. Two such groups met with
me: La Raza Media Coalition headed by Rich Bessara, and the Community Coalition for Media Change (CCMC) headed by Marcus
Garvey Wilcher. They wanted to open what they called an Oakland
News Bureau that approximately five people would staff. We would
pay them and the content they generated would be put on the air,
but the Bureau would have very little supervision from us. After that
meeting, I called Peter up in New Orleans and explained the proposed
deal.

He said, "Oh my God, that's really extortion." And I agreed. It *was* extortion. He said he didn't know if he wanted to do that.

I said, "If you don't, you better get on the next airplane because they're going to strike our application at the FCC if we don't do something." Marcus Garvey Wilcher was a guy of some repute in the state of California and he wasn't going to go away.

Peter Saves the Day

When Peter flew in to San Francisco, he immediately set a meeting with the CCMC and, because he was involved in "community ascertainment" when we bought a new station, our brother Paul went, too.

Paul Starr:

> It's just an example of Peter's resolve and courage and he would not let anybody intimidate him. We went over to Oakland, into a filthy, bad part of town. It was just Peter and I think the only reason I was really even with him is that wasn't someplace he was going to go totally by himself. I was a kid at this point, just twenty-three years old in the fall of 1971. We went to this address in East Oakland, a rundown old house, and we were told by somebody that it was the headquarters of the Black Panthers.
>
> We sat down at a table, Peter, myself, and probably four or five black men. They started telling Peter what Starr Broadcasting should do for the community. They claimed we should establish an East Bay (which is Oakland) News Bureau and I think there were scholarships involved and a string of things. But what they were getting to was they wanted us to create some jobs, and I'm sure it was for people either in their families or in their group. There was a whole laundry list of stuff that Starr was going to have to agree to do or they were going to contest the transfer of the station from Gordon McLendon to Starr Broadcasting. So we listened and listened and finally at one point Peter just kind of slapped his hand on the table and he said, "*You* know and *I* know what this is. It's government-sanctioned extortion. And we *all* know it." I was sitting there and I was thinking, *Peter have you lost your mind? We don't have a way out of this place.*

I was scared to death, and he was not. He said, "Okay what's
your price?" And they negotiated the deal. We did set up an East
Bay Oakland News Bureau and gave them several jobs.

It was a beautiful music station, elevator music, very popular
in San Francisco, and it was very profitable. But it's not the kind of
thing where you wanted somebody to come on from the East Bay
News Bureau doing a report from Oakland in the middle of all this
beautiful music. Mindful of the fact that the station was actually
licensed to Oakland, we agreed to it and we did it. It was the price
for being able to acquire the station. The whole point of the story
is that Peter had no fear. He just absolutely didn't flinch. He said
what he felt like he needed to say and that was that.

As much as we hated being forced into dealing with community
groups, our press coverage was more positive than we had anticipated.

ACTIVISTS MAKE MARK ON BAY AREA SALE
In Buying KABL stations, Starr promises extensive participation to community groups.

Starr Broadcasting Corp. committed itself to more than spending
$10.8 million when it acquired KABL-AM-FM Oakland–
San Francisco from the McLendon Corp. In agreements with
two community groups, it made some of the most far-reaching
commitments a broadcaster has yet made in the present era of
citizen activism...

And Starr told both groups it will establish a full-time perma-
nent news bureau in Oakland, which will be staffed by two
minority-group members who will be regular full time employees
of the KABL-AM-FM staff.[59]

We told the media that even though these community groups had
been filing petitions against stations in the area, we had not had any
threats, and we wanted to do "something for the community." We
also announced that we were committing to twenty thousand dollars
worth of scholarships over a three year period.[60]

A San Francisco columnist, Tim Sowell, wrote a piece that also
put our transaction in a favorable light. He said, given that CCMC's

Marcus Garvey Wilcher was a "trouble maker," "it comes as somewhat of a surprise that CCMC and radio station KABL (Starr Broadcasting), in an atmosphere of congeniality, have reached an agreement which Wilcher says should 'set the pattern for media involvement in the community.'"[61]

Sowell also pointed out that some stations were upset that these groups had held up their licenses and were not happy with Starr's success. He quoted Peter as saying, "We are concerned about the operation of our own station and are not concerned about what the others do."[62]

If these reports don't exactly sound like what happened in those meetings, there's a reason for that, as my brother Paul points out:

> Peter and Mike couldn't go out to the media and say "We've been blackmailed." They were covering themselves. That's my take on it because I was in that meeting. In the end, they had to make the deal. My recollection is that it was a stickup. We did it because we had to. We needed that station; it was a great deal. Peter and Mike wanted to get it done. That was the price they had to pay.

The CCNC didn't *try* to extort us, they *did* it, and that kind of stuff was being done all over the country at the time. That's the biggest hit we ever took, but I know other people who had similar circumstances. Interestingly, when KABL was sold to Disney (Shamrock) in 1979, the Oakland News Bureau persevered and became an institution for several years.

We were lucky, we saved the deal because the two radio stations were an incredible bargain. Pete and I got on an airplane in San Francisco and we flew to London, then to Scotland and got the money. It was a huge amount of money we were trying to get at the time and we had to get it from somewhere outside the country.

As a consequence, we were able to issue the 1972 public offering at 25 and 3/4 a share. This was compared to our IPO of 1969 that went out at 9 dollars per share. A pretty amazing thing to have happen. We used the money to pay off the San Francisco stations, and it also paid for two of our acquisitions in 1973: WWWW-FM in

Detroit and WBLG, a Lexington, Kentucky TV station. Furthermore, we had issued bonds to raise capital in 1970 and the higher stock price allowed us to pay those off, too. All of a sudden, we had a company that is getting pretty well known in the country for some major purchases, run by some very young people.

In April of 1972, the FCC approved the transfer of KABL-AM and FM to Starr Broadcasting. The vote was 5-to-2, with our old friends Robert Bartley and Nicholas Johnson dissenting...again.

Chapter 9

The Battle of New York City

NOVEMBER 7, 1974: **Mozart's Requiem—the last piece Mozart ever wrote, left on his death bed.** (Music ends)
Announcer:
> *WNCN, New York, it's 11 o'clock. Good morning. I'm Larry Miller. At this time, WNCN, New York concludes its broadcasting activities. The management and staff of WNCN thank you individually for listening and hope you have enjoyed the programming. And now by authority of the Federal Communications Commission, WNCN, New York changes its call letters to WQIV-FM, New York. WQIV-FM is owned and operated by Starr at WNCN, Incorporated… welcome to our Alternative in New York, WQIV-FM.* [63]

Opening strains of *Beethoven's 5th Symphony*, by Electric Light Orchestra (plays for thirty-four seconds). Segues into upbeat Rock guitar opening riff. (Music under, ELO vocalist sings up full):
> **"Gonna write a little letter, gonna mail it to my local DJ. It's a jumpin' little record I want my jockey to play. Well, Roll Over Beethoven, gotta hear it again today…"**[64]

Roll Over Beethoven

We were all in Buckley's office. The station came on the air and the first song it plays is "Roll Over Beethoven." I tell you, you might as well have stuck a dagger in somebody's eye because the classical music fans went nuts. *New York* magazine had stories on us every week. We kept all the jocks on the payroll, and the jocks shut the management—the owners—out of the radio station and, as I recall, they were on the air saying things like, "We're here in the WNCN studios and the classics are gone and we're just sitting here smoking pot."

The station had been one of two classical music stations in New York City. WQXR-FM was the traditional classical station and WNCN-FM focused on "breaking" classical music, although I don't know exactly what that would be. We bought it in May of 1973 for 2.1 million dollars. We had one "paid" cash customer on the air and after a year we decided to change the format to rock and roll. You could not do that without FCC permission in those days. We did it anyway. We changed the call letters to WQIV-FM, for which we did have permission. The "Q" stood for "quadraphonic" and IV stood for the number 4, as in quad, or four-track music. The jocks called themselves "The Quad Squad."

It took three days to get anybody into the station and the crowds in front of it were huge. Buckley, classical music lover that he was, said, "You know boys, for the first time in my entire life, I feel like throwing a hand grenade through my own window."

Our new rock-and-roll station took off. It was number one in the next ratings book in New York. Number one!

The Listeners Revolt—We Go to Court

But let's back up. After our purchase but before the format change went into affect, the WNCN Listeners Guild took us to court. We had letters from three governors, thirty-eight congressman, and five or six Senators against us, not to mention the petitions.

That case went all the way to the U.S. Court of Appeals in D.C. The FCC had approved our format change. We were all set to put the format on the air when the Court stopped it *the day before* the change was scheduled:

> [On October 4, 1974] The court here... put a hold on Starr Broadcasting's format switch on WNCN-FM which was due to go into effect October 5. The court is studying comments it requested from

all parties.... The FCC has generally denied hearings (which are long and costly) to citizen's groups protesting format changes. The commission has held that music and other entertainment programming is a matter for broadcaster decision... *FCC policy has held that the choice of entertainment programming is a matter for competitive marketing in broadcasting.*[65] [emphasis mine]

Remember that last sentence.

New York magazine broke the story way ahead of time that we were going from classical music to progressive rock and changing the call letters. Bill had told the magazine's publisher, Clay Felker, that he would respond when a new station had been chosen to take the classical format. But music writer Alan Rich wrote a story entitled "Mr. Buckley Passes the Buck" and Bill decided to defend himself in an op-ed that was published in *New York* on October 7. Rich produced a three-column, three-page spread with two huge caricatures of Bill. This was all in the days when magazines were not shrunk to the size of postage stamps.

Buckley summarized what he believed to be Rich's claim that,

> in order to get the FCC to approve the purchase, Starr pretended that it would continue to operate it as a classical station. [Quoting Rich] "Actually, it now turns out that WNCN's owners, the Starr Broadcasting Group, of which William F. Buckley, Jr. is chairman of the board, had charted its course when it took over the station a year ago. 'We'll keep the classical policy for a year,' the station manager at the time told a few insiders 'off the record,' 'and then we'll plead poverty and make the change...'"[66]

Bill countered that Peter Starr had promised we would "make a go" of classical music because he knew Buckley had been addicted to WNCN for years. There was no plan to ever drop the format. Bill said, in fact, revenues had come up "dramatically" in the beginning, but then dropped off after the experts he brought in to get the station off to a great start had gone back to New Orleans. He said that eventually WNCN was the only Starr property that did not return a profit. Bill's article continued,

Mr. Rich writes that the decision to alter the format shouldn't have surprised anyone, since Starr Broadcasting is "the operator of a string of lucrative rock stations around the country." Actually our most lucrative station (in San Francisco) [KABL], isn't a rock station. Management isn't addicted to rock, though much of the country is.[67]

We Win!

The U.S. Court of Appeals ruled on October 25 that we could change our format. On November 7, our classical listeners finally heard, "Roll Over Beethoven." But, we were ordered to keep our classical music handy in case the FCC were to get into the act. *Billboard* magazine responded, "The whole issue of whether the FCC should interfere with music format changes, either at the time of a station transfer, or during the license period, remains unclear."[68]

After we won, I was not worried about New York, but I was worried about the threats against the company as a whole. The Listeners Guild filed against our license renewal and it looked like the hearings would be long and the outcome uncertain, so we got out of Dodge. We had paid about $2.1 million to buy the New York station, and we sold it in a compromise for under $2.2 million to the GAF Corporation, just to get rid of the burden. We would have given it away at that point.

> *WNCN Comes Bach As Classical Station*
> After several days of transitional silence, WNCN [yesterday, August 25th] returned with the Resurrection from Bach's E-minor Mass, introduced briefly by William F. Buckley, Jr., chairman of the Starr Broadcasting Group. He said that Starr would operate the station in the classical format until its transfer to the GAF Corporation could be completed.[69]

Bill was not thrilled with the WNCN Listeners Guild and its chief counsel, Kristin Booth Glen. In March of 1975 he wrote her the following:

> You and your phony committee... have grand Jacobinical thoughts
> to pursue, and you are quite blunt in saying that you intend to per-
> secute Starr Broadcasting irrespective of whether we succeed in
> bringing good music back to New York.[70]

As it turned out, even though the station went back to classical
music, the sale was not approved by the FCC until the *last week in
April 1976*. This was because when you bought a station in those days
you were bound to own it for a minimum of three years. We were
officially granted the station in May of 1973, so the FCC, rather than
granting us a waiver on the grounds we were not going to make a
profit on the sale (which we did not), made Starr keep operating it
until the three years was up.

We Win...Again! And We Make Legal History

By 1976, Starr was out of Dodge and it was all over.

Not quite. Kristen Booth Glen and the Listeners Guild took the
format change case all the way to the U.S. Supreme Court. We won
that one, too.

The Guild argued that the FCC's policy of *not* interfering with
format changes, such as going from classical to rock-and-roll or vice
versa, was a violation of the Communications Act of 1934. The
United States Court of Appeals for the District of Columbia Circuit,
known as the D.C. Circuit, had ruled in favor of the Guild, saying
the FCC policy was indeed wrong and that "in certain circumstances,
the FCC is required to regard a change in entertainment format as a
substantial and material fact requiring a hearing to determine whether
a license renewal or transfer is in the public interest."[71]

However, the U.S. Supreme Court ruled the following on
March 24, 1981:

> The FCC's Policy Statement is not inconsistent with the Act, and
> is a constitutionally permissible means of implementing the Act's
> public interest standard.[72]... The FCC has provided a rational
> explanation for its conclusion that reliance on the market is the best
> method of promoting diversity in entertainment formats. It has

assessed the benefits and the harm likely to flow from Government
review of entertainment programming[73]... and has concluded that
its statutory duties are best fulfilled by not attempting to oversee
format change.[74]

In other words, Starr Broadcasting was responsible for a legal
precedent that radio stations around the country could make any format changes they felt were needed to be competitive in a market, and
any review of a station's format changes is "not compelled by the
[1934] Act's language or history." [75]

GAF kept the station classical for about eighteen years and in
1993 changed the call letters to WAXQ-FM/Q104.3. Guess which
format went on the air? It wasn't classical. (And yes, the WNCN Listeners Guild came out of the woodwork to oppose the change one
more time.)

The station was ultimately sold for over one hundred million
dollars. That is *thirty-three* times the price we sold it for. It's now
owned by Clear Channel.

*Peter and Michael Starr
with Walter (father),
LaCrosse, WI, 1943*

*L to R: Peter,
Marjorie (mother), and
Mike Starr while Walter
is at war, LaCrosse, WI,
1943*

Marjorie and Walter Starr, Peter and Michael, 1944

Starr Brothers, L to R: Peter, Paul, John, Michael,
Stamford, CT, 1952

Peter, Michael, John, and Paul Starr on porch,
71 Fairview Ave., 1952

Starr family home, Minneapolis, MN, 1952

L to R: Paul, John, Peter, Michael Starr, 1953

Peter's house on Wallack's Point, Stamford, CT,
two doors from Buckley's house

Michael Starr, St. Basil's High School graduation portrait,
Stamford, CT, 1958

Michael Starr, St. Basil's High School graduation,
Stamford, CT, 1958

Peter Starr, St. Basil's High School graduation portrait,
Stamford, CT, 1960

Mike Starr, Georgetown Law Center, Washington, D.C.,
1963

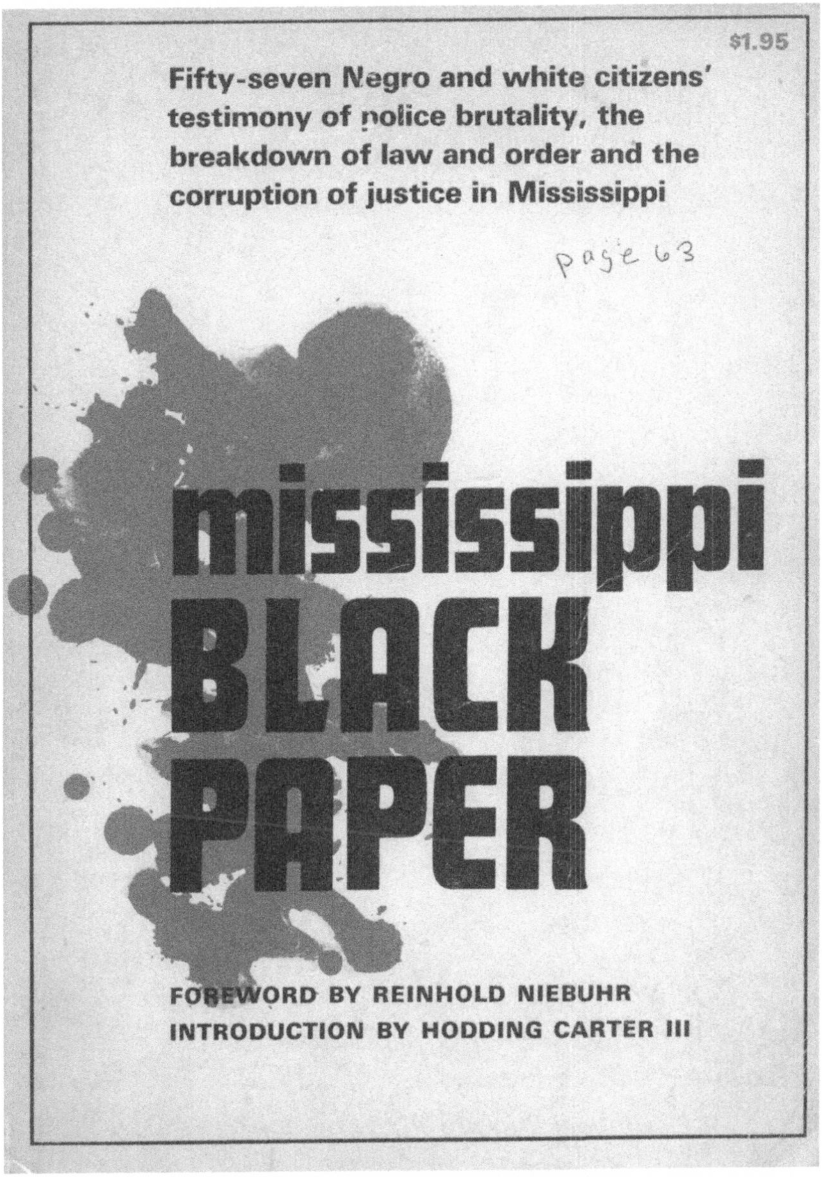

Cover, 'Mississippi Black Paper'

Michael Starr in Air Force uniform,
Lackland Air Force Base, 1966

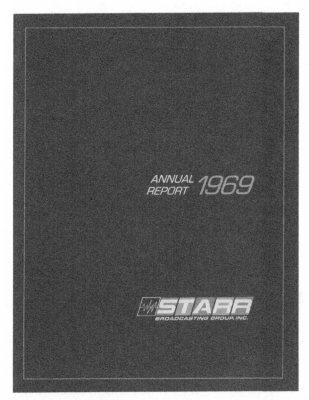

ANNUAL REPORT 1969, cover, first ever annual report

*First map of Starr Broadcasting properties
after going public, 1969*

Peter H. Starr, President of Starr Broadcasting Group, 1969

Michael F. Starr, Vice President SBG, 1969

William F. Buckley, Jr., Chairman Board of Directors SBG, 1969

Peter Starr (drawing), 1971

Peter Starr, 1970

Michael Starr, 1970

William F. Buckley,
Chairman of the Board,
1970

Gordon M. Ryan,
Secretary, 1970

William F. Buckley, Jr., 1971

Peter Starr on the 'Cyrano', 1973

'The Cyrano'

'The Cyrano' with Peter on board

Peter (standing) with Michael and Sandy at Peter and Sandy's wedding, Metairie Country Club near New Orleans, 1973

*L to R: best man Michael Starr and Peter Starr
at Peter's wedding, 1973*

L to R: William F. Buckley, John Starr, Peter Starr,
Mike Starr at Peter's wedding, 1973

L to R: Unidentified woman, Sandy Starr, and
William F. Buckley at Peter's wedding, 1973

William F. Buckley and his wife Pat at Peter's wedding, 1973

L to R: Peter Starr and Michael Starr,
Starr headquarters office, New Orleans

TM Productions, recording equipment, 1973

Peter Starr in new Kenner, LA office (film slide), 1973

Peter Starr in Kenner office (film slide), 1973

TM Productions, jingle recording session in state-of-the-art production studios, 1973

SBG officers, L to R: Gordon Ryan, Michael Starr, Peter Starr, William F. Buckley, Jr., 1973

Tom Merriman and Jim Long,
co-founders TM Productions, 1974

Peter Starr at Kenner Headquarters, 1974

Gordon M. Ryan,
general counsel and
secretary, 1974

William F.
Buckley, Jr., 1974

Starr Headquarters, Kenner, LA (New Orleans), 1974

*Michael Starr, Republican candidate for Congress,
Louisiana, 1ˢᵗ Dist, 1976*

Peter Starr at Mike's lakefront condo in New Orleans, 1976

Peter Starr "after the fall," 1977

*Last picture of the four Starr brothers together, at Mike's
condo in New Orleans, 500 Lakeshore Drive,
L to R: John, Paul, Peter, and Michael Starr, 1980*

Michael and Ruth (wife) Starr, 1980

Dear Peter:

I learned on shipboard of your mother's death, and sent you a telegram but wasn't in a position to write... Almost as along as I remember being in Stamford, your mother was that courteous, affectionate, patient voice on the telephone who mediated between us, willingly took messages, gave them to me from you. Her devotion to her family, to her faith, and to her country were only some of her attributes, all of which were known to you, some of which were known to her friends, more than enough to make her loss distinctive, and the grief of her friends real. Please do me the favor of communicating my condolences to Michael and John and Paul, to your father; and, above all, to you.

As ever

Bill

Letter from William F. Buckley to Peter on Marjorie Starr's death, 1981

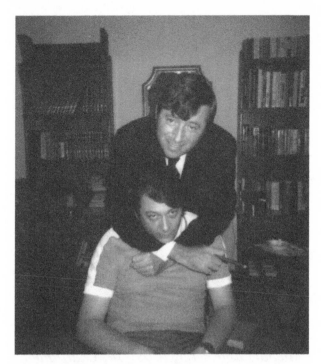

Peter (standing) and Michael Starr, 1982

Peter Starr

L to R: Michael and Peter, WDSI-TV, Chattanooga, TN, 1985

NATIONAL REVIEW, 150 EAST 35th ST., NEW YORK, N.Y. 10016
Wm. F. Buckley Jr., Editor

1/8/85

Dear Peter:

    Delighted to learn all is going so well with you commercially, biologically and otherwise.

                   Warm regards,

Note from William F. Buckley to Peter Starr

L to R: Michael, Paul, and John Starr, Slidell, LA, 2001

*L to R: Paul, Ed (first cousin), and Mike,
with Michelle (grandaughter) in kitchen,
Santa Rosa Beach, FL, 2011*

*L to R: Mike, Jim (son), and Ruth Starr on their porch,
taking a break after finishing the book,
Santa Rosa Beach, FL, May, 2015*

Chapter 10

The SITCO Theaters

From Grass Skirts to Bluegrass

At midnight on July 31, 1973, KITV was born. It had been KHVH TV Channel 4, Honolulu, owned by Lawrence H. Berger, who acquired the TV and KHVH-AM radio station in 1964. He kept the radio station and we took over the TV as well as two satellite stations on the island of Hilo, KHVO-TV and KMVI-TV.

The new KITV, for "Island TeleVision," was an ABC affiliate that also originated all Hawaii-based segments for "Wide World of Sports" in those days. That meant we got to hobnob with Howard Cosell.

In the days before satellite communications came about, programming flew out to Hawaii every one or two weeks on PAN AM airlines. All the shows seen on Hawaii stations were one or two weeks later than they were on the mainland except for the network newscasts. They would be delayed as late as midnight as the broadcasts were flown in from the mainland after they were aired live on the East coast. Until November, 1966, when ABC's satellite fed the Notre Dame–Michigan State football game to channel 4, making it the first live network telecast from the U.S. mainland to Hawaii. It was not the first live event broadcast from Hawaii, though, because on January 14, 1973, seven months before we bought the station, Elvis Presley performed the first live-via-satellite worldwide single artist concert: "Aloha from Hawaii." Only one problem. It was not seen live on the U.S. mainland because it was Superbowl Sunday.

The sale was in the works for two years before we finally got it for four million dollars. It was a money maker from the beginning, the best buy we ever made. Starr kept it until the company was sold to Disney's Shamrock Broadcasting in 1979. By that time, not only were the Starr brothers gone, but so was Bill Buckley.

Disney got such a deal on this. Buckley was an idiot to let Starr slip away. When you work all your life, as the Starr brothers did, and put something like this together worth hundreds and hundreds of millions of dollars and then... can you tell that I'm *still* mad?

After our Hawaiian triumph, in November of 1973, we bought another ABC affiliate TV station, this one in Lexington, Kentucky. WBLG-TV, which became WTVQ-TV under our ownership, was a very good buy also at two million dollars. We now had two ABC affiliates and that meant we had two stations carrying shows with Howard Cosell. A local charity in New Orleans asked if I could bring a celebrity to one of their events, and, somehow, I got Cosell.

Motown, Here We Come

In 1966, our good friend, radio legend Gordon McLendon, bought a station called WDTM in Detroit. It played mostly classical and jazz. He changed the call letters to WWWW-106.7 FM, nicknamed it "W4" and played "beautiful music" just like his KABL station in San Francisco. In 1970 Gordon switched from beautiful music to "Solid Gold Oldies." The next year it was album rock, which was the format when we bought W4 from him for eight hundred thousand dollars on May 1, 1973.

Just as we had with WQIV in New York, we broadcast the station in four-channel stereo for a while, calling ourselves "W4 Quad." When Starr owned it, it was always one of the top-rated stations in Detroit. A year after Starr departed the scene Shamrock hired Howard Stern and the next year, 1981, W4 went country. In his movie *Private Parts*, Stern depicts his leaving the station as an announcement in the middle of a record that he's quitting WWWW because he doesn't understand country music. He quickly landed a job in Washington, D.C.

While we were negotiating with Gordon about KABL and WWWW 106.7, he used to insist that we come over to his ranch. The Cielo Ranch on Lake Dallas, near Denton, Texas consisted of 5,000 acres. All sorts of people were Gordon's guests: governors, senators, movie stars (John Wayne used to film movies there), and, of course, radio people talking business.

Among other things, he had swimming pools, tennis courts, and a trampoline. He also had a big sauna that both men and women went into, and since he had mainly starlets at the ranch, it was a very interesting voyage into the sauna. One night I'm in that sauna—a naked sauna—and my wife calls the house.

"Is Mike there?"

"No. He's out in the sauna with Suzanne Somers."

From Drive-Ins to Disaster—The SITCO Deal

B.R. McLendon built his first movie theater in Idabel, Oklahoma, where his son, Gordon, grew up. It was called the State Theater, and it was the first in a chain of theaters B.R. created called Tri-State Theatres. Later, the family also started McLendon Theaters. B.R. and Gordon were partners in the movie business, but B.R. called the shots.

Eventually Gordon even got into the movie production end of the business and he came up with two science fiction monster movies. One of them, *The Killer Shrews*, was called by one critic "one of the worst movies ever made."

While we were discussing radio out at his ranch, Gordon got to talking about some drive-in theaters he knew about that were up for sale. It so happened that in 1971, Buckley, Peter, myself, and the Starr attorney Gordon Ryan had formed a limited partnership known as SITCO, which stands for Starr Investment Trust Company. It was a separate company from Starr Broadcasting, and that's important to understand. Each of us put up fifty thousand dollars to start SITCO and the idea was to make investments outside of Starr. Our first venture was an office building in Coral Gables, Florida, the same disaster that the hotel next door slid into.

Between 1972 and 1973, after we learned of the drive-in theaters from Gordon McLendon, SITCO invested in a total of sixteen drive-in theaters and one indoor theater located all around Texas. Our real estate agent was the broker for B. R. McLendon, a man named Don White. He facilitated our move into the drive-in theater business.

Don White:

> Gordon told me the Starr Brothers might buy these theaters.
>
> I talked to Peter and he said, "Yes, we're interested in that deal." The seller was a corporation in Los Angeles, the Texas Southwest Theatre Corporation.
>
> I started furnishing information to the Starrs. I chartered a Sabreliner and showed them property in Dallas, Ft. Worth, Houston, Sherman, El Paso, and Brownsville. We flew around the state and looked at all these theaters, and the Starr Brothers bought them in the SITCO partnership.

Initially it was a great opportunity. Our father, Walter, actually oversaw the running of the theaters for about a year. But by 1974, it had become a huge liability for three reasons.

First, this was the time when the Arab oil embargo hit the US. The price of gasoline doubled and people just were not driving anymore. They weren't using their gasoline to go to the drive-in theaters in particular. We hadn't made anything on the films so far, though we had made a fortune on the concessions. But all of a sudden, with the gas crisis, the customers immediately dried up and the theaters presented a tremendous cash drain.

Another problem was that some of the properties were later designated as being in flood plains, which made the land unsalable for anything other than drive-ins. Don White remembers that only one major property was listed that way, but it was problem enough.

Don White:

> As I recall, only one of these 15 theaters that I sold to the Starr brothers
> was later determined to be in the flood plain, and that was the one in
> Ft. Worth, Texas, the Ft. Worth *Twin.*
>
> The flood plain designation became a factor in real estate ownership
> around that time, 1969 through 1971. People would ask 'Is this thing in
> the flood plain?' At the time we sold that package of theaters to SITCO,
> I don't think the flood plain was a factor at all. But it became a big deal
> because the Federal Government wanted to collect those flood plain pre-
> miums from everybody so they designated about a third of the world as
> being in a flood plain. If you wanted to get financing you had to buy flood
> insurance, and it's still that way.

The third and most serious issue was interest rates. Inflation drove
interest rates. Between 1972 and 1974, the prime rate went from six
percent to almost twelve percent, which meant that we had to pay up
to eighteen percent on some of our big loans. Don White said he
firmly believes that interest rates are what crushed the drive-in theater
business.

WVUE TV in New Orleans

We had a deal with Screen Gems to buy WVUE-TV-8 in New
Orleans and, about that time, the flood plain designation started to
come up about the drive-in theaters. We were unable to complete the
WVUE purchase. However we got far into it, to the point that we
were signing employment agreements with the key people in the station. It was a great buy, and I'm sorry we were not able to finish it.
An article in *Broadcasting* in 1974 reported we had agreed to buy it
for twelve million dollars. We actually had the money, but the board
didn't want to complete the transaction until we cleaned up the other
mess.

As you will see, we weren't able to do so.

Bill's Faux Pas: the Cramdown, or the Wheels Come Off the Wagon

Buckley wanted to force the SITCO drive-in theaters, the SB The-aters, into Starr Broadcasting, which was flush with cash. But, it was a private asset. The Starr Broadcasting stockholders objected: Buckley was proposing a merger of a *theater* company that had become a cash drain into a *broadcast* company that actually had pretty good earnings. Buckley's attorney at the time wanted to do something called a "cram-down." I'll explain the term with an example: Buckley's father, Bill Sr., had a lot of family oil companies and when they had a collat-eral asset that was a problem, they would just force it into the public company. A "cramdown."

Peter and I had wanted to file chapter eleven bankruptcy and not move the drive-in theaters into Starr Broadcasting. If we put them into bankruptcy and eventually did something with SITCO—liquidate it, or whatever—we could save the company. Instead, it ended up being a major, major disaster for our broadcast company.

In June of 1975 the members of the Starr board of directors who were not part of SITCO agreed to merge SB Theaters into the parent Starr company. The banks went along with it.

And that's where the wheels came off the wagon.

Jim Long:

> The theaters were their personal investment—Buckley, Peter, Michael, and Gordon. The theaters were failing. They could not make the payments to the previous owners of the theaters, so Buck-ley headed the movement to merge the theaters into Starr Broadcasting, which was already weakened by high interest rates and a lot of recent acquisitions. But by merging the two entities, Buckley and the Starrs would be free of their personal guarantees that they had made to the former theater owners. Starr Broadcasting took the place of the SITCO partners. And it was *Starr* who was then obligated for significant payments, not SITCO. They picked up the debt that "the boys" had. And that sunk the ship.

The Starr stockholders didn't like the cramdown at all. Paul Solomon of Phoenix, Arizona filed what is called a "derivative stockholders lawsuit" against us. He only had a hundred shares, but it ultimately led to the SEC investigation of the company, which led to the end of Peter and me, the end of Bill Buckley, and the end of Starr Broadcasting.

Enter the *Cyrano*

In 1975, Bill Buckley, his son Christopher, and some of Chris's friends made a trip across the Atlantic on Bill's favorite yacht the *Cyrano*, successor to the *Panic* and the *Suzy Wong*. In June 1976, Bill wrote a book about the voyage called *Airborne*. As it turned out, the voyage took place the same month and year that Peter and I were kicked out of Starr Broadcasting by Mr. Bill himself. So it was ironic that the very first word on the very first page of Chapter 1 was "Peter." I found it even more ironic that Bill went on to heap high praise on the man he betrayed:

> "Peter," I said, late on a white summer afternoon about fifteen years ago to Peter Starr, who had sailed with me since he was thirteen when he began looking after my boat during the summers, "let's face it. Some day we'll have to sail across the Atlantic."
> "...Of course we must cross the Atlantic," Peter said... "Is there anything else we haven't done on the *Panic*?"[76]

Buckley wrote that he had an "unalterable affection" for Peter because my brother was always eager and dependable and ready to sail.[77]

Peter was more or less the captain on Bill's boats over those years. The plan to sail across the ocean was made somewhere around 1960, where Bill starts his book, but the trip didn't happen until '75. However, by that point the *Panic* was long gone.

And, oh yes, Peter couldn't make it.

As Bill explained in the book, Peter, who was now working for Starr, had "discovered the well known American phenomenon called The Business Crisis."[78]

Bill, of course, doesn't tell us what that "crisis" was, but the timing was too precise to be coincidental. It had to be the situation that was brewing over the SITCO theater properties and the huge loss of money for Starr Broadcasting. Buckley knew there was trouble ahead and he may have been thinking about throwing Peter overboard as early as June 1975. "Overboard" is the operative word.

The Cyrano—Man Overboard

The Cyrano was a luxury sailboat, sixty feet long, and Bill used to rent it out to try to minimize the loss from it every year. Starr also used it for sales trips and things like that. In 1971, we tied the boat up in New York in one of the prestigious private wharfs on the Hudson River and invited people from advertising agencies to a private party on board.

During the night, a man sat on the rail of the boat, on those thin cables. They were not made to bear weight like that, but I'm sure the man didn't know. One of the cables broke and the man fell overboard. The river was opaque at best. Nobody ever found him. I was there, but I was somewhere else on the boat and didn't see him go over. We did, however, get sued for a lot of money by the widow—$1.8 million. Bill reports in *Airborne* that the plaintiffs settled for three hundred fifty thousand dollars, three days before Bill's 1975 Atlantic crossing on the *Cyrano* began.[79]

Chapter 11

The SEC Investigation

SOLOMON V. BUCKLEY
Paul SOLOMON and Jacqueline Solomon, his Wife, as Joint Tenants, Suing Derivatively in the Right and for the Benefit of the Starr Broadcasting Group, Inc. v. William F. BUCKLEY, Jr. et al.[80]

Paul Solomon, the Starr stockholder from Phoenix, Arizona—he of the hundred shares—announced his intention to file the lawsuit in December of 1975 but, due to a problem with jurisdiction, it had to be filed again in September, 1977. Basically Solomon said that Peter, Gordon Ryan, William Buckley, and I, as the major stockholders in SITCO, knew that the company was in trouble when it merged with Starr Broadcasting. He claimed that the sale was not in the interest of SBG, but rather for the benefit of Bill Buckley, Gordon, and we Starrs.

The Securities and Exchange Commission, in part because of the lawsuit, launched a big investigation of Bill Buckley, the theaters, and Starr Broadcasting between 1976 and late 1978. It all wound up with the SEC taking Buckley and Starr Broadcasting to federal court seeking punishment for past wrongdoing and an injunction against future wrongdoing.

What follows are the events leading up to the public release of the official SEC complaint on February 7, 1979.

The Axe Falls

In addition to the Solomon lawsuit, another thing that caught the attention of the SEC was something called "The Amended 10-K." Form 10-K is a document that a publicly-held company must file with the Securities and Exchange Commission (SEC) once a year, detailing its financial results for the preceding year. If there is something wrong with it, you can make a "clarification," or an amendment.

When Starr filed its 10-K for the fiscal year 1975, according to the SEC there were all sorts of things wrong with it, including omissions and misstatements of facts.

In the words of the SEC complaint:

> Buckley departed for Switzerland after the January 23 [1976] board meeting. On February 20, Buckley was contacted by telephone by his attorneys for the purpose of securing his approval of the accuracy of the Clarification of the SITCO transaction, which was thereafter attached to the Amended 10-K filed by SBG with the Commission. Buckley *deliberately failed to listen* to the attorney's description of the agreement, but, nevertheless, gave his verbal approval to the attorneys to sign the Clarification on his behalf.[81] [emphasis mine]

In his own defense, Buckley had his lawyers, Williams and Connolly, send a memo to the SEC in the heat of the investigation of Starr Broadcasting that proved to be a classic example of Buckley's "Who, me?" defense. The memo emphasized what Buckley testified to in the SEC hearings, that until 1975, Peter Starr's success was "dazzling" and his plans had "always worked." The memo stated that Buckley had turned over the management of Starr "almost entirely" to Peter, assisted in later years by our general counsel Gordon Ryan and me. Also, the memo said, Buckley was "never active" in the management of the theaters until after they had been "crammed" into Starr. In addition, according to the memo, Buckley never tried to deceive or mislead the Starr Board of Directors, and whenever there were disclosure problems, he acted "with all deliberate speed" to correct them.[82]

Another bit of "Who, me?" came in the following section of the memo:

> In December, 1975, Buckley learned for the first time... that certain personal indebtedness of Messrs. Starr, Starr and Ryan had been assumed by Starr [Broadcasting] as part of the theatre transactions, and that this aspect of the transaction had not been adequately described in a filing with the Commission prepared by Starr management. Buckley was also led to believe that this aspect of the transaction might not have been fully disclosed to the disinterested directors in 1974.[83]

Buckley called an emergency meeting of the board in January of 1976. The members decided to make an amended 10-K to the commission where "at Buckley's insistence, transactions were disclosed fully...."

And here's where the knives came out in 1976. After the meeting, Buckley decided that "there were shortcomings in Starr management," and that Gordon Ryan and I should be fired. The memo put it this way:

> Buckley acted to encourage and precipitate the resignations of Michael Starr and Gordon Ryan. Later, in June, 1976, Buckley and the board learned of the existence of an alleged appraisal of the theater properties by Robert Richmond which established lower values for them than the appraisals presented to the board in 1974 and 1975. Upon being informed of this, *Buckley sought Peter Starr's resignation as President of Starr.*[84] [emphasis mine]

In two fell swoops, all of us were gone.

High Wind in New York

I started with what was to become Starr Broadcasting in 1965, the same year a movie called *A High Wind in Jamaica* was released. As it turns out there is a connection.

Buckley called an "emergency" board of directors meeting in New York for January 23, 1976, but I had already planned with my wife to go to Jamaica. It was very seldom that I missed a board meeting but I missed that one. When I got home from Jamaica on January 24, I got out of the car and Peter was standing at my front door in New Orleans and he said, "Don't go to work tomorrow." Well, I went to work the next morning and I started calling people on the board saying, "What the hell's going on here?"

Peter was supposed to tell me I was fired. He didn't try to shift blame to the others for firing me. He took that on himself. I knew it was not his idea to fire me. He was trying to make it sound like, when things calmed down, I could come back to work. I asked him when that would be and he said, "Four years."

I was at home in New Orleans when Peter called me to say they had had another board meeting and a lot of questions were asked.

"They put me in a room with some magazines while they considered what to do with me," he said, "and when that was over they came in and said, 'You're done.'"

They also told him that he could come back in four years.

Gordon Ryan had been fired (mostly for missing SEC filings), in February of 1976, then I was fired and then Peter in June, 1976.

The above dates are from the official SEC complaint of 1979 and from the Buckley memo to the SEC in 1978. Here's what the SEC complaint, filed February 7, 1979, had to say about the sequence of events:

> 104. During the first week of April, 1976, Michael Starr resigned as an officer and director of SBG; his resignation became effective in June 1976. In or about June 1976, Buckley secured the resignation of Peter Starr as an officer and director of SBG. Upon Peter Starr's departure from SBG, Buckley became acting president of SBG.
>
> 105. [Gordon]Ryan... resigned as [a director] of SBG in... February 1976...[85]

I will not dispute the dates, but I do know that I didn't go to work much at all after Peter gave the word at my front door on January 24.

Peter kept going to work for a couple of months after I was fired so I am not sure on which date he called to tell me he was "done." It could have been June, which is the firm belief of our friend Ed McConwell, who was Peter's personal attorney at the time. Ed says that he is certain Peter was fired at the end of June, and that he could tell Peter was in trouble drinking-wise. So Ed hopped in his private plane and flew down to New Orleans on July 1 or 2 to see Peter and sort of hold his hand, to try and get him through the crisis.

It seems to me that Peter and I were effectively out of the company for months before Peter's official firing in June. The one thing we all agree on is that Gordon Ryan was the first to actually leave the company.

Ryan had been Buckley's lawyer for KOWH in Omaha, and he's the one who did the legal work on the formation of Starr Broadcasting Company in May of 1966. He continued to function as outside company counsel until December, 1969. Then we moved the company from Omaha to New Orleans and Ryan resigned his private law firm and came to New Orleans to be part of that crew as our in-house counsel. So he was an inside member.

In the 1974 annual report, we disclosed the transaction to move the theater company into the publicly regulated company. Gordon Ryan, for whatever reason, was not current with his filing reports with the SEC and they picked up on the item in the annual report. As I understand it, the SEC began looking into our records *before* Paul Solomon filed his lawsuit.

Ryan, who spoke Chinese fluently, was always difficult to work with and kind of a violent guy. He drank increasingly over the years. His wife always blamed me for the whole thing.

I last talked to Ryan in 1992 and he was very, very mad at me but I couldn't really figure out why. He used to say that we were four men in a boat (Buckley, Ryan, Peter, and me), and if one got thrown out the other three would get thrown out. Gordon was the first one thrown out of the boat but I learned later that it was because of his failure to file the SEC stuff, which is a good and valid reason.

When Peter told me about Gordon Ryan not filing all the SEC papers, I was just astounded. I had not known about it. Nobody seems to know why he didn't make the payments and filings. Gordon always made money as a private lawyer and so I found it very peculiar that he'd made such terrible errors on Starr's behalf. Apparently it was because he didn't know anything about SEC law.

Paul Starr:

> I didn't know that much about the SEC thing at that time. I do know that we were still in the corporate office in Kenner, Louisiana when things really started to change. They would have board meetings several times a year and it had always been pretty much routine for the board members to come in laughing and joking, a very easy atmosphere. Then, at a certain point in 1975, board members started showing up with lawyers and everything was very businesslike. You could just kind of feel the tension around that place and obviously something wasn't right. It was pretty obvious that we had problems.

Jim Long of TM Productions:

> Peter and Michael were in contact with me because they knew that I was well acquainted with the new CEO, Bruce Johnson. Before Johnson was hired, Buckley had called me to say that "the boys" were being let go—he asked me specifically about Bruce Johnson and I told him what I knew. He was the president of RKO General radio stations, and I was quite surprised that Bruce Johnson was interested in his position because Starr Broadcasting was in technical default of all of our loans. It was a chamber of horrors but Johnson eventually did a good job of cleaning it up.
>
> I didn't see a whole lot of the stuff going on with Buckley. To be perfectly honest, I spent a couple of evenings at his home. He was a heavy drinker and I'm not, so Johnson and I would go to his home and Buckley would play his harpsichord after dinner and would, from the harpsichord, discuss business. In fact, he loved Peter a lot and he was very sad about what had happened.
>
> Buckley was a terrible businessman, though. For a smart guy, he was one of the worst businessmen I have ever encountered. At board meetings they passed around financial statements and he

would, like a deck of cards, kind of shuffle through them and say "perhaps Donald Alt [the comptroller] would just run it down for us verbally," because he didn't understand numbers. When we finally got refinanced and got the thing cleaned up, Buckley was gone.

After our successful refinancing of the company's debt, we had a party in New York which Bruce Johnson had planned to be the launching of the "new" Starr Broadcasting. Buckley had a few drinks in him and pissed Johnson off by conducting a tribute to Peter and Mike as being the founders, saying he was so sad about "the boys" being gone and not being present that night.

The Bloodletting

Paul Starr:

I stayed with Starr longer than I thought I would. They took some time to hire a replacement for Peter. I remember Bruce Johnson coming in for his initial meeting with everybody in the corporate office, sometime later that summer in '76, and he went through everybody and I was absolutely the last person he talked to. We had a cordial conversation but it was strained, obviously. I didn't know what I was going to do. Dick Oppenheimer was the senior vice president in charge of radio for Starr Broadcasting and he was my immediate boss. I remember Dick telling me later that summer that probably none of us had much of a future with Starr. He thought they would probably switch out everybody, but he was trying to save the situation for those of us who worked together in New Orleans. He was really trying to save the general managers' jobs too, the individual managers of each station, and he had developed a plan to move the Starr Broadcasting radio division to Dallas, Texas. Dick was going to run the radio division out of KMGC there.

He had me move to Dallas in October of 1976 and I managed that station the last six months I was part of Starr. In those months, I saw them fire one manager after another [around the country] and some of them were really good guys, very talented people. Finally, in the beginning of March of 1977, they fired Dick.

Soon afterward, I got a call from Kerry Cathcart, Johnson's in-house counsel. She told me the radio division was now being moved to Connecticut and I was welcome to make the move and continue my job there or to seek other employment. As I was making $15,000 at the time, I asked if there would be any consideration to a cost of living adjustment given the higher cost of living in Connecticut. Without even thinking, she said no, that it was for the same pay as I was receiving in Texas. It was then clear to me that this was a pro forma offer and they didn't want me. I told her "Thanks, but no thanks" and walked away from the only full-time job I'd ever had.

Everything went as Dick Oppenheimer told me it would when Bruce Johnson took over. He just systematically fired everybody in the corporation.

Chapter 12

That's Right, Chapter Eleven

Bill Bites the Bullet

You'll recall that Peter and I wanted to take SITCO, or at least the theaters, into Chapter Eleven bankruptcy but Bill refused and forced the "cramdown" instead, placing SITCO under the wing of Starr Broadcasting and thereby greatly increasing Starr's debt.

Knowing that, the following few words from the SEC might be of interest to you: "SBG caused S.B. Theatres, Inc. to file a petition for reorganization under Chapter XI of the Bankruptcy Act on December 6, 1976."[86]

Now that Peter and I were gone, Buckley decided it would be a good idea to file for bankruptcy, just as Peter and I had been urging him to do with SITCO. He was apparently convinced to do so by all the lenders and creditors demanding their money. Eventually Starr wound up giving the theaters back to their original owners or to the investment trust that had purchased the original blanket mortgage on many of the theaters.

But, while the theaters were taken into bankruptcy, Starr Broadcasting itself was not, as the new president, Bruce Johnson, told an interviewer for *Inside Radio*, a trade publication:

I think the thing that hit me hardest was there were so many problems in so many areas and all of them demanding to be number one on our list of priorities. Nobody wanted to take a back seat to the next problem so there were all these things swirling around. What we did was play fire department for a couple of weeks trying to plug the holes... but at about the time when it was most severe and most tense we were able to get three or four projects out of the way and that took the pressure off... but there was a time when I had serious doubt as to whether we'd be able to go forward on our own without the assistance of the [bankruptcy] court.[87]

The Memos—"The Smoking Guns"

All of this is interesting, but not as interesting at the infamous "Buckley Memo of 1974."

That year, William Buckley wrote a long "confidential" memo to some of his associates. That memo and another one from the late 1970s were leaked to *Wall Street Journal* reporter June Kronholz, who wrote a revealing story on October 24, 1978. An excerpt of it follows:

> "I can spot a solecism in Webster's dictionary," says William F. Buckley Jr., "but I am no good with figures. I don't understand them."
>
> So the conservative author, lecturer and talk show host portrays himself as an innocent dupe, naive about corporate finance, when questions arise about a disastrous investment by Starr Broadcasting Group Inc, the company he founded and chaired, in a string of deficit-ridden Texas drive-in theaters...
>
> And a memo that Mr. Buckley wrote in 1974 indicates that he carefully planned the [SITCO] partnership sale to Starr because he realized, in the words of the memo, "there was an imminent possibility I might go bankrupt."[88]

Buckley later described the 1974 memo as "hysterical" and "overwrought" due to the financial condition of his company.[89]

Buckley later claimed privately that Kronholz was tipped off to the SEC probe by an eccentric figure employed by Starr.

That eccentric figure was Jim Long.

Jim Long:

Yes, I did give his smoking gun memos to the *Wall Street Journal* reporter. We had to get him out of the company. The SEC investigation alone meant that we could not renew licenses because at that time licenses were on a three year schedule. If a license was not renewed, a minority group in those days could file for that license. Bill wouldn't get out because his ego was so huge and he thought it would make him appear that he was guilty.

I had copies of a couple of smoking gun memorandums. In one of them Buckley describes his version of everything that happened since my arrival on the board in 1977, and the hiring of Bruce Johnson. And of course, he'd been "hoodwinked" and this and that.

He was saying he was stuck. He felt all he could do was hang in there and spend untold amounts of the company's money defending himself because, under Delaware law (the company was incorporated in Delaware), directors are all indemnified and are provided counsel. So at the board meetings he would have a six-hundred-dollar-an-hour attorney with him almost constantly. And because of that the other directors all had their lawyers there. Having a board meeting cost twenty-five, thirty-five, forty thousand dollars for a company that was in technical bankruptcy. He was pushing the company further into the red because we were paying all his lawyer bills. I decided on my own that the best thing I could do was expose him.

I had this memo where he admits that he made a mistake in trusting "the boys," which would be his way of explaining that he was hoodwinked. I gave it to June Kronholz at the *Wall Street Journal,* and she created an opening round of front page stories that put a lot of pressure on Buckley to do something.

The Hearings—Mike Takes the Fifth

At the SEC hearings on Starr Broadcasting, which were held in the summer of 1978, all of the major players were called to testify, including Bill Buckley, who appeared on June 6, 7, and 8, and August 3 and 4. All the players were called except yours truly.

I took the fifth amendment and did not testify. Everybody was looking for a scapegoat. I was executive vice president and treasurer of the company. I had a lot of power, but I was not the president. I was a member of the board. Peter and I usually were very much in agreement, especially on this theater situation. Buckley's main concern was making sure that he had his reputation intact, to be able to do the columns and the speaking engagements and all that kind of stuff, so he would have done anything, and he *did* do anything, in order to insure that somebody else had their ticket punched instead of him.

Buckley under the Table?

Ed McConwell:

> Stanley Sporkin was the chief enforcement counsel for the SEC at the time. Bart Sacher was the attorney who was in charge of the depositions in the Starr case.
>
> During his testimony I think Bill Buckley made Sporkin mad by giving what some might call evasive answers. Steve Umin, one of Buckley's attorneys, is a very good lawyer and was probably pretty tough on Sporkin, and I think there was an aggravation going on. At some point, Sporkin started investigating the family corporations that Bill Buckley's father had started. This had nothing to do with Starr, but was started during the middle of the SEC Starr investigation.
>
> This came from Peter, I didn't see it, but I understand that Bill *passed out* during his deposition and I think they had continuances that were not acceptable to the SEC and it got a little rowdy. There have been rumors that Bill slipped under the table. I don't know about that but he did pass out. I think he did come back and finish the depositions.

The Complaint
SEC SAYS WILLIAM F. BUCKLEY BROKE LAW TO AVOID
BANKRUPTCY FOR SELF AND OTHERS[90]

The Securities and Exchange commission handed down an official complaint against Starr Broadcasting, its officers and Board of Directors, and the Columbia Union National Bank on February 7, 1979. Before it was announced, most of the defendants had agreed to a consent decree, stating they did not admit or deny the allegations in the Commission's complaint and did not admit to any wrongdoing.

In the complaint, the defendants were accused of violations of the Securities Act of 1933. Just one example, focusing on the inaccurate 10-K form, is the following:

> Item 15(a) to the Form 10-K did not state:
> a. that the purpose of the SBG-Sitco [sic] transaction was to assist Buckley, Ryan, and the Starr Brothers in avoiding personal bankruptcy;
> b. that the theatre properties had been unprofitable from the outset...[91]

The total complaint comprised fifty-six legal pages. In signing the consent decree, Buckley agreed to pay $1.4 million dollars in cash and stock, and he did not admit guilt. In fact he maintained, "I am not guilty, I never committed fraud." He also agreed not to sit as a director on the board of any public company for five years. He told the *Wall Street Journal*, "I haven't any intention, given what I now know about the technical responsibilities of a director, of ever serving as a director of a public corporation."

On the same day the SEC released its devastating complaint on Starr Broadcasting and William F. Buckley, the man himself issued a rather large press kit to the media. It contained an interesting Q&A session. He called it a "background statement" but, apparently, it's Buckley doing one of his famous interviews... with himself.

Q: What happened to the company counsel [Gordon Ryan] who filed the misleading reports?

A: It was suggested he resign, which he did.

Q: And then?

A: A revised 10-K was filed disclosing every material detail that had been left out of the previous version.

Q: Did you at any time knowingly withhold any information to which you were privy from anyone who under the securities laws had a right to such information?

A: No.

Q: Why are you signing a consent decree?

A: Because the alternative is litigation over a period of years at an expense of hundreds of thousands of dollars and thousands of hours of time with the outcome uncertain because the SEC's regulations obstinately decline to distinguish between technical and substantive guilt.[92]

At the time of the consent decrees, both Peter and I pleaded poverty. In an affidavit, I said I was "without any funds, tangible assets or property, real or personal, with which to pay any disgorgement claims which may be asserted" against me by the SEC. I claimed medical expenses "in excess" of ten thousand dollars. I also mentioned three hundred dollar a month expense in child support (for the two children Ellen and I had adopted during our marriage). I also revealed that my estranged wife was seeking an increase in those payments. I said I did not anticipate having "in the immediate future any regular employment with which to pay my debts."

Peter wrote a letter to the SEC citing one hundred thousand dollars in attorneys fees and expenses as a result of the SEC investigation and the Solomon v. Buckley suit, saying he was willing to waive all claims for reimbursement of the money if both cases were solved by compromise. He also added a nice little touch at the end:

"This agreement shall be null and void if either Solomon or the SEC case is tried. In the event of trial, I will seek attorneys' fees and expenses applicable to the case that is tried."

Chapter 13

Sale to Shamrock

Who's the Boss?

With the company losing money and the "boy geniuses" gone, the only one left from the original Gang was Jim Long, and he eventually found out what it was like to be lied to by the boss:

> Both Bruce Johnson, the new president who replaced Peter, and Bill Buckley promised me that Starr would sell TM Productions back to me and my partner by returning the stock which we had earned. But it wasn't happening. They were dragging their feet because TM was really generating a very good cash flow at that point, and Buckley wanted to clean the company up, get it out of its default position with the banks, and get rid of the lawsuits and the SEC investigation. That was his excuse for getting rid of Peter and Michael—that he was cleaning out the barn. He had to do it for the shareholders' benefit because he was a wonderful guy.
>
> But Buckley remained, and he put three of his Yale classmates on the board. He didn't want to get off the board and give up his position, and with three directors in his pocket he had total control of the board. If he left the board, he felt it would be an admission that he was a wrong-doer, that he had committed fraud. Which he had.
>
> Bruce Johnson and I joined the board and we engineered the sale of WCYB-TV in Bristol, Tennessee for $8.6 million and WLOK-AM for eight hundred thousand dollars. Also, Starr sold Alan Torbet Associates and Arlington House Publishers, all of this to raise money to shore up the sinking ship.

This helped toward bailing the company out, but the SEC investigation went on... and on... and on. The solution was to sell the company to someone else but Buckley didn't want to do that.

Buckley finally agreed to sell to someone—a third party—and would leave the board. Doing so would allow the licenses to go through because they wouldn't be transferred as long as he was the chairman of the company or had anything to do with it on a day-to-day basis. He agreed to do this only if I would also resign, because he thought I was his nemesis in creating all of these problems for poor Bill. I agreed to do so as long as his classmates also left the board at the same time he did.

We both resigned from the board on August 31, 1978 when we agreed to sell the company to Shamrock. However, the remaining board members voted me back on the board in October of 1978, along with three of my nominees. This was extremely important because it gave us an insurance policy—we would be able to control the company if Disney's Shamrock deal didn't close for some reason.

In the first part of 1978, the trade publications, as well as the *Wall Street Journal*, had been full of buzz about the imminent demise of Starr Broadcasting with such headlines as "Starr Principals in Mood to Sell"[93] and "Suddenly Starr Broadcasting Is in Demand."[94]

But then, "Disney Agrees to Acquire Starr."[95]

A Starr Turns into a Shamrock

The final curtain dropped down on Starr Broadcasting when, on June 7, 1979, the Federal Communications Commission approved Roy Disney's Shamrock Broadcasting purchase of Starr Broadcasting, giving 22 million dollars to Starr stockholders. Shamrock then took the company private. Roy was the nephew of Walt Disney, and he formed Shamrock for the sole purpose of purchasing Starr. The commission also approved two other major acquisitions:

The Starr-Shamrock merger was approved by the commission with little discussion. The commission staff saw no reason that the Securities and Exchange Commission complaint filed against a number of Starr principals, including columnist William F. Buckley, should delay approval. Most of the principals have reached settlements with the SEC, which, among other things involve their payment to Starr stockholders of $1.8 million in cash and stock.[96]

The FCC could have decided that the SEC ruling against Starr only a few months before that was a problem, but the FCC staff actually reasoned that the money which Starr/Shamrock was ordered to pay stockholders by the SEC settlement was a positive factor and would help Buckley meet that obligation.

Good for Bill.

Not good for me and Peter. And ultimately not good for Jim Long.

Jim Long:

> After the sale I had a five year contract with Shamrock.
>
> I quit after 3 months.
>
> TM never left Starr Broadcasting, because even though the new heads agreed to sell the company back to us, they didn't keep their word. Bruce Johnson became the president of Starr, and then was made president of Shamrock after they bought the company. At that point they looked at the money TM was making and they were not willing to sell, so they bought out my stock and Tom Merriman's stock, and the employees' stock for about six million dollars. The company was worth at least ten.

These are the properties that were transferred in the sale of Bill Buckley's media kingdom to Shamrock's magic kingdom:

KXLR-AM, North Little Rock, Arkansas
KABL-AM-FM, Oakland/San Francisco, California
WBOK-AM, New Orleans, Louisiana
KYOK-AM, Houston, Texas
KUDL-FM, Kansas City, Missouri
WWWW-FM, Detroit, Michigan
KMGC-FM (formerly KDTX-FM), Dallas, Texas
WTVQ-TV, Lexington, Kentucky

KITV-TV, Honolulu, Hawaii
KHVO-TV, Hilo, Hawaii (Satellite)
KMAU-TV, Maui, Hawaii (Satellite)
LE-BO (Music and broadcast accessories), Queens, New York
TM Productions, Dallas, Texas

I ask you, dear reader, in that list, did you see any properties that were *not* acquired by Peter and Michael Starr?

Bill's Legacy

Bill Buckley's raison d'etre in life was basically rhetorical: theories of political endeavor, interviews, telling of his experiences at Yale, etc., for which he wasn't graded. But there is something absolute about a business equation and how business is conducted that reflects on character, the individual engaging in it, his capability in his position, and how he responds to a problem or crisis. Even if the average person does not understand the issue involved, the average person does understand character and that affects a legacy.

The early stages of Watergate didn't affect Nixon because the true story wasn't out there. Over the passage of time, had the Buckley thing not ended the way it did—that is, being able to toss a lateral pass to somebody else and get out of the play—if it had gone on a little bit longer, it definitely would have had an effect on his legacy.

So what *was* Bill Buckley's legacy vis-a-vis (to use one of Bill's favorite phrases) Starr Broadcasting? Bill's image was bright and shiny to the masses, but it was quite tarnished to those who knew him personally or had to deal with him in business. They say "no man is a hero to his butler." That was the case with William F. Buckley, Jr., to his protégés.

Ed McConwell:

> Bill Buckley was very charming person one on one. I think he was a little bit abrupt at times, but I think he was a good person. A very talented, very smart individual. He and Peter were the best of friends. It was like a father and son relationship.

Even though Buckley was not putting up any money, they were using Bill's name. And the bank in Kansas City would do backflips to get Buckley in there. He would come in and give presentations, and the bank president just bent over backwards, so proud of what he could do—it was helping him feather his cap in Kansas City society.

I really felt Bill was kind of going along with the program. I felt also, at the time of Peter's death, Bill really was very sorry that this had happened. He had just been protecting himself and he really just jumped ship on these other three guys. He had the assets but he maybe didn't have the cash to develop what he needed to.

I didn't have animosity toward him. He was just too weak to stand up and be counted. He hung Peter and Michael out to dry, there's no question about that. Bill Buckley was not loyal to his friends.

Jim Long:

First of all I didn't like his politics, so I should put that out there. I didn't even know what *National Review* was. But he had that charisma that Bill Clinton and Elvis and a lot of people like that had. In his own way, he was so charismatic. He was a creative guy who had a great ability to get his point across, as we all know from the television shows. He never met an argument that he couldn't get into and probably win, or at least come out looking good. The problem is there was no substance behind it when it came to business. I watched him in these board meetings, and I was no sophisticated businessman, but I could see that to be able to look at a simple P & L [profit and loss] or to really analyze a problem was beyond him. That's how he got into the radio business in the first place, and put Peter in the radio business, by being sold a bill of goods and buying a radio station for way more than it was worth.

My observations of him over a period of a couple of years was that he didn't *get* the radio business and the business of Starr Broadcasting. He didn't grasp it; he faked it. Anybody talking to him would think he knew all about radio and what was going on with his group when, in fact, he knew no more than what somebody else told him.

In his heart and soul Buckley was a creative guy. He would love to just get on the airplanes and get out his portable typewriter and write. He told me on a couple of occasions that he could be in a plane flying and writing for the rest of his life.

He knew that selling those theaters to Starr Broadcasting was bailing him out. It was bailing him out more than anybody else because he owned more stock. And he probably had more net worth by far than Peter, Mike, and Gordon, who just had their Starr Broadcasting ownership as their assets at the time. Filing bankruptcy for them might mean they would lose their stock but Bill Buckley being involved in a bankruptcy is beyond what he could deal with. He came across as a guy with an inheritance in oil and lived in a big house and acted like he had a lot of money. He had a TV show, but the *National Review* was losing money all the time and just cleaning his clock.

Still, he couldn't let it go.

John Starr:

I was not connected with Starr Broadcasting when Mike and Peter were cut loose. I had some conversations with them, but they were so engulfed in the mess. I would call them to see how they were doing, but I didn't really talk to them and didn't see them a lot because it was pretty devastating, especially when they had to surrender their stock.

It was awful. They had built that company, and Buckley basically turned on them and blamed everything on them.

Why did Buckley do it? He did it to save his ***. Save it from bankruptcy. If they didn't bring SITCO into Starr they would have had to bankrupt SITCO and Buckley didn't want that on his record.

Peter was not holding up well. He was pretty devastated. Peter was not one to show his emotions. Mike was more that type and Peter held it in. But he certainly felt betrayed.

Thoughts at Sunset

Until 1976 we thought Bill Buckley walked on water.

After, we couldn't believe that what was happening was orchestrated by Bill to get rid of us. All of a sudden, it hit us. I have actually figured out more of what happened this year while working on this book than I had ever puzzled through before. And it is just sadness galore. It cost me a marriage, my job and assets. I had a hard time getting started in business again. I managed to on my own, though I didn't think I could. But Peter, he was just absolutely destroyed. He always had a drinking problem to some extent, but Pete had bought a house a couple doors from Bill's on Wallack's Point in Stamford, Connecticut. So it wasn't like they didn't see each other. As I recall, Pat Buckley would not allow Buckley to go over to Peter's house. Sometimes they would meet on the beach and they would talk. Bill told me after Peter died that the whole deal was the worst experience of his life, but *he* set it all up. I was told there were a couple of times when he appeared at company events and went on and on about how they should not forget Peter and me because of what we did, that they wouldn't be here today if it weren't for Pete and Mike Starr. People like Bruce Johnson didn't like that one bit.

Johnson didn't end up very well. The last I knew, he was somewhere in the Midwest with a couple of radio stations. He really hit the bad times. He had a very interesting resume, and even Jim Long said that Johnson did a couple of pretty good things.

Early in his stewardship, Johnson asked to meet with Peter and me in Atlanta at the airport and Peter refused to go. Johnson wanted to review the properties and their financial performance because he didn't think that we were getting good enough financial performance out of these stations. But we *were*. The problem wasn't the electronic media; the problem was the celluloid, the drive-in movie theaters.

Consider the price we paid against the performance we got out of every property we bought. We bought major market FM's for around one hundred thousand dollars each. The New York FM was sold for about two hundred million dollars. We paid two million for the ABC affiliate in Honolulu and that was later sold for two hundred million, too. There was no way in my lifetime I could ever recreate the kind of wealth that I had accumulated in those days.

Politics was Buckley's driving force in life, but he was torn between shoring up his political image and justifying the "money machine" he needed to keep that image afloat. On the politics side, Bill was famous for taking the leaders of the GOP out of the wreckage of the Goldwater debacle of 1964 and guiding their ragtag army from the 1964 abyss into a movement that won in 1968. Bill once recalled to us the "rush" he felt as he took a private meeting with President Nixon in the Oval Office.

In the end, Buckley's motivations required the sacrifice of the Starr brothers, the designers of his media wealth. His desire to keep up his image won over any gratitude toward us for the synergistic empire that we had built for him. I remember one night in the '70s, after we had been defrocked, Bill took Peter and I on a tour of the imperial baths that Bill had built under his Connecticut residence. And where did the money to build that come from? Revenue from millions of on-the-air commercials that we generated.

Peter was struck by the savagery of our departure. We talked about it often afterwards. All we ever talked about in those years was "The Fall of Rome."

I had wanted to take legal action against Starr Broadcasting and Buckley for our firings, but Peter just didn't have the stomach for it. And, for the same reason, Peter would have never written this book

Chapter 14

Life after Starr

I Get into Politics

In 1974, the Republican party asked me to run for state senator from New Orleans in a special April election, caused by the resignation of state senator Adrian Duplantier so he could take a judgeship.

I had a long-time interest in politics, as my childhood and early adulthood testifies, and a very interesting thing happened: I won the Republican primary. I had convinced New Orleans city councilman Jimmy Moreau to drop out so I was in by default on the GOP line. An African-American candidate—Sidney Barthelemy—won the Democratic primary. So all of a sudden, here I am with all my bouquets and certificates and everything else, and I'm the White Racist Candidate against a black guy who had gone to a Catholic seminary for a while.

Sidney Barthelemy was a class act in my opinion. I never wanted to run against him. I expected one of the other candidates to beat him in the Democratic primary but that's not the way it was.

In the general election of April 30, 1974, Barthelemy beat me in what I thought was a fairly close race, 57% (9,106 votes) to my 43% (6,743 votes). He became the first African-American elected to the Louisiana Senate since reconstruction. Sidney was then elected to a full term, and in 1978 he resigned to run for New Orleans City Council. He later became the second African-American mayor of the city of New Orleans, serving two four-year terms.

Gerry and Jimmy, and Me

By 1976 I had left Starr Broadcasting and wasn't doing much of anything, and my wife Ellen and I were separated, so it was a pretty rough time.

I had talked with long-time Democratic congressman F. Edward Hebert, and he said he would call me when he was ready to retire. He called me in Jamaica in 1976 during my famous vacation and told me he was not going to run again.

I decided to run for Congress, but after Watergate I could see what was going to happen in 1976. No Republican was going to win an open seat for Congress. Nevertheless, after I threw my hat into the congressional race, President Ford appointed me to the Federal Energy Administration and I thought that job had a better shot at turning into something than running for Congress that year, so I dropped out of the race. There was even a formal press release:

> FOR IMMEDIATE RELEASE – SEPTEMBER 21, 1976
> Office of the White House Press Secretary
> **THE WHITE HOUSE**
> The President today announced his intention to nominate Michael F. Starr, of New Orleans, Louisiana, to be Director, Intergovernmental, Regional and Special Programs, Federal Energy Administration. He will succeed William W. Geimer, who became Deputy Assistant Secretary of State in April, 1976. Mr. Starr has been Acting Director of Intergovernmental, Regional and Special Programs at FEA since July, 1976...[97]

On September 27, 1976, I was endorsed by the Senate, 98-to-0.

The FEA later became the Department of Energy. I didn't enjoy the job when I saw the politics of it all. The country had terrible energy problems at the time, and if a governor came up and was unhappy with the allocation he was getting or something like that, I was the guy that had to talk to him.

When Jimmy Carter beat Ford in the 1976 election, I stayed on. I just sat around. Nobody was doing anything and I figured that, until I found something else I wanted to do, what the hell. I remember telling the *Southern Illinoisan* newspaper some years later, "Most of the [Ford] people in my office resigned, but I decided to see what would happen. They didn't 'find' me until May, 1977. Then one Thursday they told me my farewell luncheon would be Friday at noon."[98]

I really came away from that with a fundamental understanding of oil dependency. One time in the early '80s, Jimmy Carter was at a fishing lure show downtown and I just happened to run into him and I said, "Mr. President, I was one of your guys at the department of energy." We talked for a while and he said, "I think we did some good."

In 1978, the Republican Party wanted me to run again. I didn't want to so Bob Livingston said he would like to run. He asked me to come down and endorse him at his announcement party. I went down to New Orleans and I was supposed to introduce Bob.

My sense of humor kicks in at strange times and I called him over and said to him, "Bob, I've decided to run after all." I thought it was funny because I had no intention of running, but here we are at his party, one minute before he's going to announce, and I tell him I'm going to run and that I can't endorse him.

He was very gracious. He said, "Mike, you go right ahead."

I said, "Bob, I'm kidding."

He about buckled over. We've been lifelong friends, but we still have very different senses of humor.

Congress Again

I actually did run for Congress, this time in Illinois in 1992. It was really a messy Chicago-type campaign with some real gangsters. I won the Republican primary, getting the same number of votes that Bush got. But I lost big in the general election to the incumbent Democrat Jerry Costello, 71.2 to 28.8 percent.

I thought about trying it again a few years ago, but I didn't think I was prepared to dedicate the time to it that I would have thirty years back.

Back to Broadcasting—Ventures on My Own

SOUTHERN BROADCASTING CORPORATION—1982

WMOD-TV started from a construction permit for a new television station in Orlando, Florida. We put it on the air "from scratch" in July of 1982 as an independent TV station on Channel 43. There were two congressman shareholders involved. The call letters were going to be WKNA, which stood for Nelle Ayres, who was the original Project Coordinator for Southern. They were changed before we went on the air to WMOD, for Melbourne, Orlando, and Daytona.

We came into the deal with only six months before the permit expired, and there was a big problem with getting land and building a tower in that short a time period. We actually went on the air with six hours to spare before our permit expired.

Programming consisted of film features and network series in syndication. National sports and other programs were aired off satellite. The plan was to originate local news in our studios and to develop future shows with NASA focusing on their space programs. I sold my interest in Southern in order to buy WDSI-TV in Chattanooga.

SOUTHERN STARR BROADCASTING—1983

The development of Southern Starr Broadcasting is a very important element in the "rescue" of Peter and, to some extent, me as well. It would normally go here in this time line, but I am saving that story for the following chapter, "Camelot Ends," which tells of Peter's final adventure in broadcasting.

WDSI in CHATTANOOGA—1985

WDSI-TV was a UHF television station on Channel 61 in Chattanooga, Tennessee. I, and a partner by the name of Lou Donatelli, bought it in 1985 for five million dollars. It was one of the first Fox affiliates in the country and one of the first to carry Joan Rivers. The station also carried first-run syndicated sitcoms that had recently been on the air. For example, we carried *M*A*S*H* and *Benson*. We sold the station to a company in Pennsylvania, in which I still have an interest that won't be liquidated until Donatelli dies.

Our biggest deal at that station was the launching of *Star Trek* "TREK-A-THON 1" on July 5, 1986. Three stars of the *Star Trek* television series—George Takei ("Mr. Sulu"), Nichelle Nichols ("Lt. Uhura"), and James Doohan ("Scotty")—were beamed to the Chattanooga Convention and Trade Center to mingle with what our press releases called "Trekkies." Apparently, more serious fans like to be called "Trekkers" (although *Star Trek* creator Gene Roddenberry is alleged to have said "It's Trekkies. I should know, I invented the thing.")[99]

The whole event was enveloped by twenty-four hours of *Star Trek* programming on Channel 61, which kicked off the syndicated broadcast of the series.

Paying It Forward

In the summer of 1988, I got to thinking about passing on some of the things I learned about broadcasting to a new generation. A friend of mine showed me a school bulletin that listed an opening in the radio-television department at Southern Illinois University at Carbondale. I applied and got the job.

My subjects were broadcast and cable promotions, and broadcast law and policies. I got so involved that I became the faculty adviser to the local chapter of Alpha Epsilon Rho, which was the student broadcasting society. It was at SIU-C that I met the lady who helped me produce our PBS documentary *Mississippi, America* about the Freedom Summer of 1964.

Broadcasting...Again!

GOODSTAR BROADCASTING—1997-2000

Goodstar Broadcasting consisted of a collection of fourteen AM and FM stations in Kansas. The venture proved successful for us—we called ourselves the Goodstar Network—but it was very difficult to manage because we were spread all over central and western Kansas. You name the city and Goodstar had a radio station there: Oberlin, Colby, Liberal, Dodge City, Great Bend, Salina, Garden City, and more. We had formats ranging from Real Country, Adult

Contemporary, and Classic Hits to News/Talk/Country to Oldies, Spanish, Spanish Oldies, and Easy Listening. The more stations you advertised on, the lower your ad rates.

My friend Ed McConwell took off his lawyer hat and put on his pilot hat to help us publicize one of our prize catches in the deal. We had pulled off a coup by signing up Oliver North (of Iran-Contra fame), to do a radio program. We decided to do a promotion trip for North to visit the various cities where the stations were located. Ed got hold of a Cessna Citation that he and his son flew to pick up Oliver North and me, and they flew us around to the different stations, including those Dodge City and Colby, Kansas. We made numerous stops. Then we went out to Denver International Airport and dropped North off. Oliver North got on another plane and went home. Ed was thrilled to be the pilot on that trip instead of the lawyer.

WBJJ GUMBO 104.5 FM in BATON ROUGE—2000

This was another station with an expiring construction permit that I bought for a pittance. It was an FM and there weren't any stations left in Baton Rouge, so my plan was to go on the air with one of the formats of Guarantee Broadcasting. They had a bunch of stations in Baton Rouge. They were in a black format and so I chose to use the same. I had one disc jockey and we ran the station twenty-four hours a day for six months with *no commercials*.

My son Jim, whom I'd adopted when I married his mother Ruth, was named General Manager. He had graduated with a BA in Radio-TV from Southern Illinois University at Carbondale, where I had been an instructor. Within three months of Jim's becoming General Manager of KILS radio in Salina, Kansas, the station had a thirty-nine share of the ratings and a 300% increase in revenues. Like father, like son.

Our promotional material stated: It is our mission to provide a radio station for the community that mirrors the diversity and flavor of South Louisiana's rich local culture...that is best reflected by local cuisine, particularly gumbo.

Hence, Gumbo 104.5 FM.

The music consisted of local artists such as Fats Domino and Rockin' Sidney, and national favorites like Michael Jackson, Diana Ross, Otis Redding, Tina Turner, Stevie Wonder, and the Four Tops. Our ratings just came out of nowhere, and Guarantee bought it from me for lots of money. We built it in early 2000 and sold it in December, 2000. I owned it for less than a year but what a year it was.

DELTA STARR BROADCASTING—2000-2009

Delta Starr Broadcasting had two stations. One was KTIB-AM in Thibodaux, Louisiana. It had a great signal on 640 AM with 5,000 watts and it covered a good bit of the state. The other station was KANE-AM, licensed to New Iberia, Louisiana. It broadcast in French for the Cajuns of Southwest Louisiana.

WGSO 990 AM in SLIDELL, LOUISIANA—2007

The most recent of my broadcasting projects was WGSO, a 1,000 watt AM with a tower on top of one of the New Orleans downtown hotels. That tower was supposed to be moved closer to our target population, but it never happened. We saw the need for public service programming on a commercial radio station on the North Shore of Lake Pontchartrain in the New Orleans area. However, our Metro New Orleans investment group, consisting of about nine people, was never on the same page with regard to the mission of the radio station, where it ought to be located, and how it was to be operated.

I really thought, and I still do, that if you had something anchored in Slidell on the North Shore with a lot of localism for a bedroom community of New Orleans, it would be valuable. We tried and we were making excellent progress in the rating books at the beginning, but there were substantial misunderstandings and miscommunications between the partners. The net result was that nobody was happy. There were two camps: one of them wanted to aim the programming strictly at North Shore listeners, the other thought we should have more general programming and target South Shore listeners as well.

While 1,000 watts could be heard quite well in New Orleans on the South Shore, it wasn't as strong as it needed to be for our target listeners across the lake, especially at night when we had to reduce power. We wanted a local-oriented morning show, which we achieved. People were expecting a strong news presence but we didn't deliver it, partly because no one locally wanted to take the job of news director.

We paid a lot of money for some veteran marquee New Orleans broadcasters, who were familiar names to the listeners, and that created a lot of publicity without spending much on promotion. Doing so gave us an early shot in the arm, but sales were disappointing and the dream of WGSO-990 AM lasted only about a year.

Chapter 15

Camelot Ends

Peter Fights Depression and Leaves the Game Too Soon

In 1983, someone told me about two FM stations for sale for five million dollars—a steal. I sent a certified letter to Bank One in Columbus, Ohio and made an offer that the seller, General Communicorp, accepted. The stations, one located in New Haven, Connecticut (WPLR-FM) and one in Orlando, Florida (WHLY-106 FM), had about as much power as you could get in FMs at the time. They were making money, but the owners were in so much trouble they just couldn't get out of it. The bank accepted my offer of five million and suddenly I was Southern Starr Broadcasting. Years later, the Orlando station alone sold for twelve million.

Peter and I didn't see much of each other for several years after Starr Broadcasting's demise. He moved to New York, then got a management job at a TV station in Toledo so he moved to Ohio. He also ran the Consolidated Rail Network (CONRAIL) for a while. The whole train system in America had started to break up, but when CONRAIL was formed in 1976, the government took some of the regulation shackles off and allowed the railroads to make some money. Amtrak had been formed for passengers in 1971, and now, in 1976, CONRAIL was for non-passenger operations.

Peter later managed WHOM-FM in Portland, Maine, which covered six states from its transmitter on Mt. Washington in New Hampshire, but it considered itself to be a Portland station. (In the mid-1960s, the station, under different call letters, had been owned by "Tonight Show" host Jack Paar.)

Peter was broken in spirit and very depressed. At Starr, I had always called Peter, "Mr. President." When I knew that I had won the bid for what was to become the "Southern Starr" stations, I offered Peter the Southern Starr presidency.

Peter had been good enough to include me in the Omaha deal with Buckley way back in 1966, so when I had this opportunity, I wanted Peter to come and run the stations. He said he didn't think he knew anything about handling a deal anymore, but Peter came to my house and stayed for three days. Ruth, Peter, and I talked into the night about the situation, but Peter was not the brother and partner I had known. Still, he agreed.

Once Peter took over as Southern Starr's president, he rode his bike to my house every Saturday to give me a "President's report" and the station was a huge success. I was chairman of the board until I bought a TV station in Chattanooga in 1985. Peter did a great job and the group was very successful.

Just to show you how the more things change the more they stay the same, we got stung in another property transaction, this time at Southern Starr. We were buying a station in Myrtle Beach, South Carolina on the Grand Strand. The owner was a big-time embezzler and thief, but we didn't know it then. As soon as he had our escrow money, he sold the station to somebody else. He sold it more than once. It never did go through the commission but it took a bunch of lawsuits to get our escrow deposit back. He was a very, very polished professional con man.

In 1991, Peter invited me on an expensive Caribbean cruise with his wife Sandy and my wife Ruth. Peter looked really terrible. The constant fights Peter and Sandy got into took a toll on him. The cruise doctor even ordered Peter to stay in doctor's quarters because of his fights with Sandy. She really knew how to wind his clock.

We had not seen much of each other since 1985. I had begun teaching in 1988 at SIU and by that point was chairman of the Radio-TV department, which got most of my time.

The cruise was in January. Peter and I had a long conversation aboard ship. He told me he was going to divorce Sandy and that she knew it. He spent half the cruise telling me all about the situation. When he drank, he talked about it even more and a lot of people in his neighborhood must have known. Sandy used to try to get information out of me about what people thought of her, then said things like, "Don't you think I'm a good wife?" I didn't answer those questions.

Then Peter had a heart operation. He should have had a second one but he refused. He also stopped taking his cholesterol medicine because it interfered with his drinking. And it killed him. Peter and I talked a couple of times after the cruise but I regret, and always will, that we never had a chance to continue the long conversation we'd started aboard ship.

After being fired from Starr, my brother had been chronically depressed. But soon after he came on board with Southern Starr, I said to him, "Well, Pete we have another shot at the big time."

"No," he said, "we've had our shot at the big time." In point of fact, this time we were on the right track again.

And then he died.

July 21, 1991. Age forty-nine.

At six in the morning, my phone rang. I was in Illinois. It was Kathy Renyo, Peter's secretary. She had previously worked for me.

"Peter died last night," Kathy said.

Sandy would not take my call.

When I got to Peter's home in Winter Park, just outside Orlando, Sandy gave me her version of how Peter died. She told me he had thrown up and fallen to the floor. She said that, as he lay there, he said to her, "Please come and hold me." As she spoke I noticed that, on the floor, was an envelope that had been hastily torn open. It read, "Peter Starr: Last Will and Testament."

It occurred to me that Sandy was more interested in the contents of the will than in the fact that Peter had just died. I was told she had not called 911 or any other emergency number.

I arranged for an autopsy to be performed on Peter to see if we could get an official cause of death. I had known he wasn't doing well.

All sorts of possibilities raced through my head, like that Peter's heart condition could easily have been exacerbated by the anger produced by his marriage.

Peter's drinking problem would have been part of his life with or without Sandy, but he used to be able to retreat and recover when he was having a rough time. With Sandy, he could not do that. He would come home every day from work and nothing was ever cooked for dinner, which was a major expectation in those days. My brother had to drive to the bars around town to find Sandy. It was a stormy, pressure-filled marriage, and perhaps it was simply a matter of time before Pete's heart gave out. Was it his heart? We won't know for sure because, as I found out when I got to the funeral home, Sandy had cancelled the autopsy. Peter was gone now, and the lives of everybody close to him were changed forever.

The board of Southern Starr appointed a successor, but as the Orlando Sentinel reported, "[Robert] Long, who already was chairman, took on the additional responsibilities of chief executive officer. Yet the board chose not to appoint him president—in deference to Starr." Quite a tribute to a very nice guy.

Sandy virtually froze me out of the funeral. She warmed up at the funeral lunch, but I later realized that she wanted me to use my contacts to help with her career post-Peter.

One such instance occurred in 2004 when the Bush administration brought Sandy to Louisiana to work on a special 72 hour voter turnout campaign. Because I was politically connected, she wanted me to make some phone calls and introductions for her, which I did. Then the Department of Education offered her a job because she had such a "terrific broadcast background," which she really didn't. She was simply married to Peter, who was now gone. They asked her to develop a nationwide campaign of public service announcements, but she didn't have the expertise to do it and they let her go. They thought she misrepresented herself.

Aside from the times when she wanted my help, I hardly ever heard from Sandy. Until she got cancer. In her later years she used to tell me that she could not talk to me because I looked too much like Peter.

Sandy moved to D.C. She always promised to leave Peter's money to me, though she did not. I spoke at Peter's funeral, but not Sandy's.

Camelot Is Over

Shortly after the assassination of John F. Kennedy at the age of forty-six, his widow, Jacqueline, told an interviewer:

> "At night before we'd go to sleep, Jack liked to play some records; and the song he loved the most came at the end of this record. The lines he loved to hear were:
> 'Don't let it be forgot, that once there was a spot, for one brief shining moment that was known as Camelot'"
> "...there'll be great presidents again... but there'll never be another Camelot.... This was Camelot.... Let's not forget."[100]

That's how I, and the people who went through it, feel about what we had at Starr Broadcasting. Whenever a memorable era comes to an end, people think of Camelot, either the stage musical or the life of JFK, and relate it to their own lives. There'll never be another time in broadcasting history to equal what we experienced. For us, 1964 to 1976 *was* Camelot, but we didn't think of it that way until Peter died.

Now, it was all over. Just like JFK, Peter didn't even make fifty years old.

I think of him every day.

Memories of Peter

Ed McConwell:

> When Peter got fired, Buckley's attorneys were the ones who convinced Buckley that Peter had screwed him and had rolled over on him and that Peter was the bad guy. Peter immediately got drunk out of his mind, for a pretty extended period of time. I got on my plane that night when I found out about it and flew to New Orleans and spent several days with him. But he was just in

miserable shape. I don't know if he and Bill ever had another rational conversation about the whole thing.

J. Daniel Mahoney was an attorney in NYC, an organizer of New York conservative groups and he was Bill Buckley's personal attorney. My impression at the time was that he orchestrated Buckley's deciding that Peter and Michael Starr had done something wrong and had not been loyal to him. Mahoney started the process that resulted in the termination of Michael and Peter. He was really the guy pulling the strings. What he told Bill Buckley to convince him to go along with that process, I don't know, but it did not have a very pleasant result for Peter and Michael.

There was a suit filed in 1983 and I'm sure I prepared it. Basically, it argued that Mahoney wrongfully caused Peter Starr to be fired. Ultimately it was dismissed without being processed. Peter felt that Mahoney had given bad information to Bill Buckley that caused him to be fired.

Paul Starr:

I remember times when Peter and I would have dinner and a few drinks in the French Quarter in New Orleans, and he would tell me what all he was doing. At the time, FM radio had not come of age—it was still developmental in 1971 and 1972. In most markets, AM radio stations were still the top performers. He said KDTX-FM in Dallas and KUDL-FM in Kansas City "are gold mines. They're gonna be worth a fortune."

National Airlines and Peter's Typewriter

John Starr:

One time I went to the airport to pick Peter up and I met him as he was coming off the flight. When we went to get his luggage, he discovered that his portable typewriter, which he had received as a gift from Bill Buckley, had been destroyed. And I mean destroyed. It was all smashed up, and Peter was boiling mad.

We went over to the section of the terminal where the airline counters were and we saw a sign that said "National." Peter had flown on National Airlines, so when we got about ten feet from the counter he *threw* the typewriter at the attendant behind the National counter, and he said, "You just bought a typewriter!

It flew about ten or fifteen feet, and the attendant was like, "What in the hell is going on here?" and he grabbed the typewriter. He caught it, it was amazing. He said, "Sir, we're National *Car Rental.*"

So, Peter grabbed the typewriter and said, "Nevermind!"

All these years later I can still envision it, and when he threw that typewriter I was really concerned he was going to get arrested. I'm going, *Holy cow, is he angry.* But after throwing the typewriter at the wrong guy, he cooled down. He realized he almost hurt somebody who had nothing to do with anything.

So, we walked over to the National *Airlines* desk and Peter proceeded to tell them it was a very important item in his life and they had destroyed it and asked how they were going to make it better. The guy was nice and friendly as he explained to Peter that he would have to make a claim at the baggage office. Eventually Peter told me he received a check for sixty or seventy dollars or whatever those things cost in those days, but he could not replace the fact that Buckley had given it to him.

Paul Starr (rebuttal):

I was there too, and it's my recollection that Peter just slammed the typewriter down on the counter. I don't think he threw it. I can, however, confirm the rest of the story.

Peter's Driving

Paul Starr:

Peter was not a great driver to ride with. He could scare you a lot. We were working in Camden, NJ and we were going to drive to Philadelphia. The highway went through a tunnel and I don't know how Peter did it, but somehow he got us on the wrong side of the road and we were in the tunnel before we realized that there was a whole lot of traffic coming right at us. He threw the car into reverse. I did not know a car could go that fast in reverse and it fish-tailed backward as we were trying to get away from three or four lanes of

traffic coming at us. He got us out of the tunnel and he hopped
it up onto the median grass just seconds before the cars whizzed
past us.

Chapter 16

Where Are They Now?

Bill Buckley

Bill's memorial mass during Lent of 2008 was said in St. Patrick's Cathedral in New York City with Reverend George Rutler, his long-time friend, presiding. Rutler wrote in a blog that Bill said the Rosary every day at least once and more often if possible. He attended mass every week (in Latin, when he could find it) and went to confession on a regular basis.[101]

Fewer than three months before his death on February 27, 2008, Buckley wrote a column about how he and his wife Pat, when they were twenty-seven years old, vowed to give up smoking cigarettes. They had both smoked since they were fifteen. After one day of it, he wrote, they flipped a coin. The winner got to continue smoking and the loser had to give up the habit. Bill lost.

Buckley wrote "I stayed off cigarettes but went to the idiocy of cigars... and now suffer from emphysema." [102]

He and Pat were married for another fifty-three years, until she died from what Buckley assumed was "sixty years of nonstop smoking." He himself died less than three months after his smoking-confessional column appeared.

Bill was such a good Catholic that, in the end, he decided he would *not* commit suicide, even though he was in terrible pain from the emphysema and other ailments. "If it weren't for the religious aspect, I'd take a pill," said Buckley, according to his son, Christopher.[103]

Christopher revealed this in a book he wrote about a year after his father's death, entitled *Losing Mum and Pup*. But Sam Tanenhaus almost beat him to the punch. Tanenhaus, who had claimed for the last fifteen or twenty years that he was writing an authorized biography of Bill Buckley, called Chris to tell him that he was planning on writing a story in the *Times* about Buckley's suicidal thoughts. Chris writes in his own book that he replied to Tanenhaus that his father obviously told him that *only* for the biography, and that if Tanenhaus wrote the story, Chris would cut the author off from any further access to his father's confidential papers.[104] Chris worried that, if it showed up in the media only days after his father had died, the headlines would have been a "nightmare."[105]

Tanenhaus held off on the story, which allowed Chris to break it in *Losing Mum and Pup*.

Howard Kurtz (now with Fox News) was, at the time of Chris's book's publication, a staff writer for the *Washington Post* and reviewed the book.

> [Christopher Buckley] sums up his painfully intimate portrait in *Losing Mum and Pup* this way: "He was impossible. She was impossible. And sometimes their impossibilities acted like great magnetic force fields." Which is to say, William F. Buckley and Patricia Buckley had a stormy marriage and an equally volatile relationship with their only child....
>
> "There were times," he admits, "when I happily would have traded them for Ozzie and Harriet."[106]

Tanenhaus resigned his post as editor of the *New York Times Book Review* in 2013, five years after his dust up with Chris Buckley. Tanenhaus, at this writing, is still an "at-large" writer for the *Times* and continues working on his Buckley biography.[107]

My Brother John

John left WBOK in New Orleans in late 1974 or '75, then went to WNOE for about six or seven months and I helped him buy WMOB-AM in Mobile in July of 1975.

He worked for me in Florida at a TV station I owned for a while. When Peter and I left Starr, John went to work for various companies and finally wound up in Melbourne, Florida working for a newspaper. He married a lady who collected animals. She started building this zoo at home and she had some horses and some ducks. She had one particular horse that liked to go inside their house. You'd be sitting in the living room and the horse would come in, look around, and go over and sit down on the couch.

After Peter and I left Starr, but before it was sold to Shamrock, John, believe it or not, tried to buy WBOK from the new CEO, Bruce Johnson

John Starr:

> I actually had a deal cut. I was going to buy the station for eight hundred seventy-five thousand dollars. Johnson didn't know who John Starr was. I called him because it was reported they were going to sell off all the stations. I said, "Would you be interested in selling WBOK?"
>
> He said, "Yeah, absolutely."
>
> We went back and forth. He sent me financials, and it was just like KOWH. It was in decline. When I was at WBOK, we were doing about a hundred thousand dollars worth of business a month. But, now it was down to about fifty or sixty thousand a month. I made an offer, we went to contract. We never got to transfer of the license. The sale never went through because he finally figured out who John Starr was!
>
> He said, "Are you Pete and Mike Starr's brother?"
>
> "Yeah," I said.
>
> "How in hell can I sell it to you?" I told him that the name of my company is Bay Broadcasting. He said, "Yeah, but you own more than ten percent of the company."
>
> I said, "Yes, I do. I own a third of it."

"I can't sell it to you."

He thought he would be accused of making an inside deal with a member of the Starr family. I had never told him I was 'the Brother'. I had just told him I was John Starr from Mobile, Alabama and I was the President of Bay Broadcasting. I think at some point we sued him for specific performance. We ended up settling for about fifty grand because they told us they would just wear us out legally.

I talked to Bill Buckley a few times, after the breakup. One time I actually called in to Larry King's radio show in the late '70s, while Buckley was a guest. I said to him, "Bill, this is John Starr, from Shippan Point and the *Panic* and all those good things."

"John, how are you?" he said.

We talked about the old days, with the *Suzy Wong*, and the *Panic*, and Stamford. Not about Starr Broadcasting.

I said to myself, "I'm not going to last very long on this phone call so I'll go ahead and ask him what happened to him and Peter." Just a general question. But I was too late. All of a sudden, they cut me off, and Larry said, "Evidently, you know this guy."

Buckley said, "Yeah I do." So I'm just wondering if Buckley gave him the signal to get rid of me. At first he was very gracious on the phone, but then I think he realized who I was.

In 1994, I got a job in Gainesville. I started attending the University of Florida in 2008 and graduated in 2013 with a PhD in communications. I worked for a company called Asterisk for many years. I had built a very successful news talk and sports talk package, and then and they sold out to a company called JVC out of Long Island. I parted ways with them in March 2014. I joined Marc Broadcasting the next month. I'm now the sales manager of NEWSRADIO 980/720 and I'm the senior account manager for the other stations: Pulse 106.9, HANK 101.7, The Buzz 100.5, and Magic 101.3.

I still love it. I absolutely do. And I'm still teaching at the University of Florida in Gainesville.

My Brother Paul

After I left Starr in March 1977, it took a few months, but with Dick Oppenheimer's help I found an opportunity as a general manager of KIKZ in Seminole, Texas. I went there, to the farthest corner of West Texas, to run my first radio station from 1977–1980. It was in Seminole that I met my wife, got married, and did well enough running the station that, when I told the owner that I was leaving for a larger station, he tried to sell it to me for the money left on his note. I turned him down and headed thirty miles across the border to Hobbs, New Mexico.

For three years I served as the Sales Manager of KYKK/KZOR in Hobbs for Noalmark Broadcasting, then transferred to El Dorado, Arkansas to do the same job at Noalmark's KELD/KAYZ station from 1982–1986.

It's funny how West Texas grows on you. When I got my first look at Seminole in July, 1977, I thought to myself, "One year, that's all I can give this." I thought it was the most God-forsaken place on the planet. Now, in February, 1986, I was being given the opportunity to return to the same general area as vice president/general manager of KYKK/KZOR. Over the next twenty-five years we built the two stations into a group of six stations and grew revenues from under half a million to $3.2 million per year.

As the last Starr in Starr Broadcasting, who was no longer wanted by that company, I enjoyed a thirty-three year career in radio broadcast management and sales, developed the most profitable operation in Noalmark Broadcasting Corporation's twenty-seven station group, and in 2011 I was named to the New Mexico Broadcasting Association's Hall of Fame.

While I made my career and my living with Noalmark Broadcasting in the state of New Mexico, I will never forget the excitement of those early years in the '70s with Starr Broadcasting Group. There is no doubt in my mind that my brothers were ahead of their time. With the liberalization of broadcast ownership rules in the 1990s, several publicly owned broadcasting companies grew to own hundreds of stations nationwide. Starr Broadcasting Group in the '70s was the precursor of these huge groups and, had it survived to operate in the new world of broadcasting, it could well have been a Gulfstar, a Citadel, or a Clear Channel.

Ed McConwell

I have continued to practice law after Starr, all over the United States. I do aviation law primarily, as well as corporate litigation. I had my own office in Overland Park, Kansas, near Kansas City, since 1966 and from time to time I've had lawyers employed with me. I was there until 1997 when I moved to Mission, Kansas and bought the building where I am located now. Since 1989, my daughter Laura has practiced with me.

Eighty percent of what I do involves airplanes. I'm seventy-three years old but I don't intend to retire. I may slow down, but I won't quit.

I have been flying for fifty years. Peter and Michael were way ahead of the curve on broadcast facilities. I flew them in one of my twin engine airplanes in 1969 down to Mexico to look at a cable TV network. And we also did the Oliver North tour in the late '90s.

I fly a Piper Mojave and a Twin Commanche. I own the Commanche and I owned a Cessna 414 for eleven years, until I sold it last year. I have a lot of planes available to me, but own just the Commanche now.

I have practiced law all over the US, including Alaska, and I have clients in Australia and Germany and have had pilot's licenses for both countries. Linda, my beautiful wife, and I have been married fifty-three years and have been friends since we were little. We have three children, two girls and a boy, and nine grandchildren.

Jim Long

In 1980, after Jim left Shamrock Broadcasting—in effect leaving Starr—he went out on his own and founded FirstCom Broadcast Services, providing promotion and music production. In 1980, Long formed Long-Pride Broadcasting with country singer Charley Pride. They also purchased radio stations in Wichita, Kansas and Beaumont, Texas.

In 1984, radio stations across the country gave a big thank you to Long for introducing the first ever compact disc (CD) production music library, Digital Production Library. No more vinyl taking up space in the production room. Eight years later, FirstCom put its entire music catalog online, allowing radio and TV production staffs to find their music instantly.

Formed in 1992, Jim's Honest Entertainment record label produced albums exclusively for established artists, including Pat Boone, Charley Pride, Toni Tennille, and Jack Jones under the Gold Label name. The label was sold in 2001 to Pat Boone.

Since 2013, Jim has been an active investor specializing in music catalogs through his family-owned Telos Holdings, Inc.

Jim also is chairman of Crucial Music Corporation, an online music licensing company that places music in films and TV shows. Long also serves as executive chairman of the library division of Elias Arts.

Sian and Michael, Jr.

In my first marriage we adopted a girl we named Sian, which is an Irish name, and the boy we named after me, Michael Starr. They've both had problems in life, but they have done really well. Sian now has three children, and her first child, Caitlin, gave birth to my first great-grandchild in June of 2013. In 2002, Michael went to college and got a master's degree. His wife also had a master's. They have two children.

Mike, Jr. went out to New Mexico to teach at a Navajo reservation school, which I thought was a laudable thing to do. He's done pretty well and now he's a 'muckity muck' at a big school in Albuquerque, where people do their senior year in high school and their first year in college at the same time.

Miss Ruth

My secretary was a good friend of Ruth's. After my marriage to Ellen fell apart, I met Ruth and we started dating. We got married in 1980. I picked her because she worked hard, she is smart, and she was organized, unlike me. And she had a great son, Jim, whom I adopted. He lives with us in the carriage house at our home in Destin, Florida.

I like how Ruth tells the story of our meeting, so I asked her to handle this one:

Donna Miller, who had been Mike and Peter's secretary, was my best friend and I met him through her. I was spending the weekend with her and he dropped by with his children and that's when we met. Monday night, Donna called me and said "Mike told me he is gonna marry you.

I said, "I'm engaged?" and I laughed, because I had just met the guy.

She said, "Don't laugh, I've never known Mike to say he was going to do anything that he didn't do."

We met in November of 1979. He was smart, he was funny, he was cute. He was attentive and just very charming. My son, Jim, was ten when I met Mike. Jim always loved Mike. They really took to each other. Mike and I started dating and we married in June of 1980 in a Baptist church in Metairie, Louisiana.

I didn't know anything about what had gone on when Mike was with Starr. I only knew that Starr was no more. I knew who William Buckley was. Starr Broadcasting was on Howard Avenue in New Orleans by then, not far from where I worked. One time—years before I ever met Mike—Donna called me and said "Ruth, come on over, we'll have lunch and I'll introduce you to Bill Buckley."

I told her, "I wouldn't walk across the street to meet Bill Buckley." I was never very fond of him as a public figure.

As the years went on, Mike told me about the situation with Buckley and Starr Broadcasting. It messed up his life. It messed up a lot of lives.

What impresses me about Mike is his brain. He's so smart. And glib. Mike is very funny. He has a dry wit. A lot of people will miss it. After years of knowing him, he'll say something and I'll laugh, and others in the room won't get it. Then they'll realize he said something funny. Only somebody as smart as he is could be as funny as he is.

I don't think he'll ever retire. He keeps saying he will. He kept saying he was going to retire after the beginning of 2015, but that's been pushed back some. I don't think Mike will ever just sit and not do business.

Chapter 17

To Set the Record Straight

The Best Example of Why I Wrote This Book

When Bill Buckley died in 2008, his obituary was published by every major news organization in the world. Outside of obits, columnists and bloggers and major writers all came up with their takes on the life and career of the man. But, there was one column published which was not so much an obituary as it was the remembrance of Douglas E. Hall, who had come into contact with Buckley in 1976, shortly after Peter and I were fired.

Hall's 2008 column in the *Bergen News* of Bergen county, New Jersey, was an update of a piece he wrote in 1976 for his own radio industry newsletter called *The Hall Radio Report*. Here is part of what he wrote in 2008:

Buckley's Trial in the Boardroom

William F. Buckley, Jr. [was]… I learned some 30 years ago, a paragon of probity, and a man who could, and did commit a major blunder that involved a fine levied against him by the Securities & Exchange Commission (SEC).

Mr. Buckley and I crossed paths in a series of events that began in the 1970s when I was writing and publishing my nationally distributed radio management newsletter, *The Hall Radio Report*. It began when I wrote a report on the Starr Broadcasting Group

(SBG), a publicly traded company, headed by Mr. Buckley, who, at that time, was chairman of the board.

The report was an exposé of a business transaction, which the SEC would later find to be a violation of the law.

In apparent gratitude for my writing this report, Mr. Buckley invited me to a banquet at the New York Yacht Club in Manhattan where he presented me with a plaque commending my investigative reporting...[108]

The story went on to discuss the growth of Starr's radio business, and the relationship between the Starr Brothers and Bill Buckley:

[Hall:] According to my original story and subsequent SEC complaint, certain SBG officers, directors and others engaged, as the SEC put it, in a five-year course of business ultimately resulting in the inflated purchase price by SBG of 17 theaters from a partnership owned by the principals of SBG, including Mr. Buckley, President Peter Starr and Vice President Michael Starr.

Mr. Buckley's involvement with the Starr brothers seems to be an illustration of the old adage, no good deed goes unpunished.

For it seems as if Mr. Buckley wanted to lend a helping hand to the brothers...

Mr. Buckley, perhaps a father figure to the Starr boys, became an investor in the company headed by Peter and Michael Starr...

Acting on a tip, I called the SBG offices and requested a copy of the 10K form SBG had to file with the SEC. All I did was have a phone conversation with a secretary, and I soon came to learn SBG was in trouble. I received a sheaf of assorted papers in the mail...There seemed to be conflicting figures. I put it all into a story, which was my big scoop. *Broadcasting* magazine picked up the exposé a week later...The award Mr. Buckley gave me stated: "The Starr Broadcasting Group Distinguished Achievement Award. For major contributions to the survival and rebirth of the Starr Broadcasting Group, this award is presented." Apparently, Mr. Buckley appreciated my scoop as a wake up call to allow him to make what amends he could and cut his losses in a bad situation...[109]

Douglas E. Hall:

> I would consider the story basically *un*favorable about the manage-
> ment of the company, which consisted of the Starr Brothers. I think
> the story made Buckley look rather stupid. The impression I got,
> and I think the reason he gave me a plaque for it, was he was not
> paying attention closely enough to the business and he was kind of
> like an innocent bystander. He convinced *me*, at least.
>
>   It seemed like it was ineptitude all the way around.
>
>   I guess the impression I started out with of Buckley vis-a-vis
> the Starr Brothers is that he was an "I'm above it all" kind of high
> class guy, and "I'll take these boys under my wing and help them
> out," and that's why I said "no good deed goes unpunished."

Buckley may have convinced Hall that he was an innocent
bystander, but it's not so. Buckley was in on the acquisition of the
drive-in theaters from the beginning. He came up with the down payment and I know he made at least one of the interest payments to the
real estate investment trust. The idea that he woke up one morning
and said, "Gee, what the hell are those guys doing with all those drive-
in theaters?" is just wrong. As for the nonsense about merging them
into the broadcast company, Peter and I resisted that and got put out
after it did happen. I think in later years Bill reflected on his responsibility for what happened to us.

I always thought it was a *National Review* award. Hall's story does
paint a picture of a different Buckley than anybody else knew. And a
fellow who would conjure up a thing like an award from a company
under investigation? If *National Review* had given the award, that
would be one thing, but for Starr Broadcasting to give him an award
for tearing up Starr Broadcasting? I just don't get it.

He did take us under his wing but people like Hall don't recognize
the fact that it was Peter and I who built the company. I have said
elsewhere in this book that, over the years, Buckley maybe put up one
hundred fifty thousand dollars for everything we bought. Millions
more—everything else—was leveraged by Peter and me. This would
have been a multi-million dollar company and maybe still flourishing

if it weren't for the theater deal. That's why Peter and I were so proud: we built the company even without Buckley's financial input.

Douglas E. Hall:

> It's my assessment and observation over the years that the wealthy never part with their money readily. Buckley gave one hundred fifty thousand dollars. That's chump change, and he let the Starrs struggle and work hard, and he probably figured that would make them better people. That's probably what Buckley envisioned that they should do and become.

I wondered why, after all this time and all this information, Hall would still be taking the position that he took, not wanting to admit that he made a mistake in the story.

Hall says, "I was unaware that I made a mistake. To this day I don't know that I made a mistake."

I don't like to let the thing go completely because it's another example of the grandiose measures Buckley would have implemented to insure that the blame was not dropped at his door. I think that's an important part of the story.

Did Hall go easy on Buckley because Buckley gave him an award? Hall says no, that he got the award *after* he published the story:

> The award implies I had the right story, that my story was okay....
>
>   I never interviewed Bill Buckley, and I never interviewed either of the Starr brothers. I went strictly on the information that was sent to me when I placed a call to Starr Broadcasting and got all these attachments to the legal filings... I think there were originals and some were photo copies.

Did the secretary send him only information favorable to Buckley and unfavorable to the Starrs? Hall says "No."

> I don't think so. I mean, she responded so quickly. I got it two days later in the mail. Maybe she thought I was a lawyer representing

somebody. I didn't misrepresent myself. I told her who I was and why I was calling. I was amazed that she sent it all to me. It was the whole story, so that's how I wrote the story...

I had no relationship with the Starr Brothers and very little relationship with Buckley.... [Mike] knew Bill far better than I. I met the man once, when he handed me a plaque.

It would have been nice if I had talked to them [the Starr brothers] and talked to Buckley. I was a one man band putting out this newsletter every week and it wasn't the only news I was covering. Everybody's got their own story. You know the old country song, "We all live in a two story house. You've got your story and I've got mine."

Hall is the greatest example of why I wanted to write this book and why I worked on it all these years. As I said in the introduction, *I want people to know the real story.* Hall and many others don't know the truth, and I'm hoping that some opinions will change upon the reading of this book after thirty-nine years. People have told me I waited too long to put my story out there, but I believe it's never too late. Writing a memoir takes a lot of organizing, soul searching, and, I guess, a lot of living. The only person who knows when the time is right is the one telling the story.

For me, the time is now.

Epilogue

A friend of mine recently recalled an episode in the lives of the Starr brothers, which I now believe to have been a big clue we all missed to our future at Starr.

It was the adventure of the Columbia Union National Bank (Chapter 4: Omaha). I had cultivated that bank and they were a personal lender to Peter and me. So, when Bill asked me to arrange an unsecured loan for fifty thousand dollars, I did so.

I was pretty much out of the picture until, as you may recall, Buckley refused to pay the note, saying he never signed it. When Bill did this, he threw Peter and me under the bus in favor of his own priorities, whatever they may have been at the time. The bank relationship was beyond repair. This was a fifty mega ton hit on us.

After that, when Bill needed sacrificial lambs, Peter and I were ramped up again for the bus.

Why were we surprised each time? In my view, it had to be misplaced trust in an amoral man. Buckley was for Buckley and no one else. He was just setting us up. I haven't yet figured out why, unless it was just in his nature.

The "bloodletting" of 1976 crushed not only the souls and emotions of Peter and me, but Mom and Dad as well, Walter and Marjorie Starr. I had a sudden heart attack in 1980, followed by heart surgery. I recovered, but Mom was, by then, suffering from lung cancer. She told me she was "ready to go," and she did just that in 1981. I slept on the floor in her bedroom toward the end, hoping I could do some good. But, of course, I could not.

When I founded Southern Starr Broadcasting in 1983 and invited Peter to come run it, my brother rented a home close to mine in Melbourne, Florida. Dad had decided to move down there so we could all be together again, even though Mom could not be part of it.

The night Dad arrived, we were all having dinner at Peter's home. Dad stood up from the table and dropped dead.

The ending of Starr Broadcasting and the careers of Mike and Peter Starr weighed very heavily on Mom and Dad. They had been one hundred percent sold on Bill by his frequent visits to our home in Connecticut and his solicitous phone calls. Neither of them could ever understand how their friend Bill could have treated their sons so badly.

Neither could their sons.

Michael F. Starr, March, 2015

****

This book was written to show the absolute dedication of two young men who built a significant national broadcast company in a nanosecond with little or no capital to speak of, though much was promised by their business partner.

They were rewarded with Buckley's betrayal and destruction. The company they built was sold, piecemeal, for hundreds of millions of dollars, beginning shortly after they were forced out of the business they themselves had built.

Michael and Peter crawled their way back. Through financial affliction and domestic upheaval, they survived with major personal damage.

From the graveyard to the poorhouse, Pete and Mike rebuilt their fortunes and families—but not their reputations. Not completely.

Together and apart.
Inseparable then and now.
The spirit lives on.
Remember them please... Michael and Peter Starr.

Notes

1. "Peter H. Starr, Radio Executive," *Orlando Sentinel,* July 23, 1991, accessed March 1, 2015, http://articles.orlandosentinel.com/1991-07-23/news/9107230411_1_starr-broadcasting-winter-park.

2. "Buckley's Cruiser Missing," *Stamford Advocate,* August 21, 1960.

3. Howard Kleinberg, "Split over 'Tractors for Freedom,'" *Miami Herald,* July 24, 2000.

4. *Attorneys Brochure on Mississippi Law.* Jackson, Mississippi: National Lawyers Guild, Committee for Legal Assistance in the South, 1964.

5. Michael Starr, *Mississippi Black Paper* (New York: Random House, 1965).

6. Douglas Martin, "William F. Buckley Jr. Is Dead at 82," *New York Times,* February 26, 2008, accessed April 4, 2014, http://www.nytimes.com/2008/02/27/business/media/27cnd-buckley.html?pagewanted=all&_r=0.

7. Reid Buckley, *An American Family: The Buckleys* (New York: Simon & Schuster, 2008), 27.

8. Ibid., 53.

9. Ibid., 47.

10. Ibid., 52-53.

11. Douglas Martin, "William F. Buckley Jr. Is Dead at 82," *New York Times,* February 26, 2008, accessed April 4, 2014, http://www.nytimes.com/2008/02/27/business/media/27cnd-buckley.html?pagewanted=all&_r=0.

12. William F. Buckley, Jr. and Christopher Little, *WindFall: The End of the Affair* (New York: Random House, 1994).

13. William F. Buckley, *Miles Gone By: A Literary Autobiography* (Washington, DC: Regnery Publishing, 2004), 115-120.

14. Douglas Martin, "William F. Buckley Jr. Is Dead at 82," *New York Times*, February 26, 2008, accessed April 4, 2014, http://www.nytimes.com/2008/02/27/business/media/27cnd-buckley.html?pagewanted=all&_r=0.

15. Buster Brown, "Skull and Bones: It's Not Just for White Dudes Anymore," *The Atlantic*, February 25, 2013.

16. Bob Colacello, "Mr. and Mrs. Right," *Vanity Fair*, January 2009.

17. Daniel McCarthy, "Conservatism's First Family (*An American Family: The Buckleys*) (Book Review)," *The American Conservative*, July 28, 2008.

18. Douglas Martin, "William F. Buckley Jr. Is Dead at 82," *New York Times*, February 26, 2008, accessed April 4, 2014, http://www.nytimes.com/2008/02/27/business/media/27cnd-buckley.html?pagewanted=all&_r=0.

19. Paul Zeilbauer, "Two Old Foes, Buckley and Yale, Signal Truce," *New York Times*, May 19, 2000.

20. From Buckley's forward to *American Spy* by E. Howard Hunt, a former CIA operative and Watergate conspirator who died in January, 2007. Hunt, E. Howard, and William F. Buckley. *American Spy: My Secret History in the CIA, Watergate and Beyond.* (Hoboken, New Jersey: John Wiley & Sons, 2007), ix, xi.

21. Douglas Martin, "William F. Buckley Jr. Is Dead at 82," *New York Times*, February 26, 2008, accessed April 4, 2014, http://www.nytimes.com/2008/02/27/business/media/27cnd-buckley.html?pagewanted=all&_r=0.

22. John B. Judis, *William F. Buckley, Jr.: Patron Saint of the Conservatives* (New York: Simon & Schuster, 1988), 135.

23. Ibid., 146.

24. Geoffrey Kabaservice, "The Tea Party's Godfather (*Living on Fire: The Life of L. Brent BoZell, Jr.*) (Book Review)," *The National Interest*, April 22, 2014.

25. Sam Tanenhaus, "Q&A on William F. Buckley," *The New York Times*, February 27, 2008.

26. Robert D. McFadden, "William Rusher, Champion of Conservatism, Dies at 87," *New York Times*, April 18, 2011.

27. Douglas Martin, "William F. Buckley Jr. Is Dead at 82," *New York Times*, February 26, 2008, accessed April 4, 2014, http://www.nytimes.com/2008/02/27/business/media/27cnd-buckley.html?pagewanted=all&_r=0.

28. Associated Press, "Reagan Snubs 'Cinderella'—Misses Party," December 7, 1980.

29. Lawrence Van Gelder, "Judge J. Daniel Mahoney, 65, Founder of Conservative Party (Obituary)," *New York Times*, October 26, 1996.

30. Sam Tanenhaus, "The Buckley Effect," *New York Times*, October 2, 2005.

31. Lawrence Van Gelder, "Judge J. Daniel Mahoney, 65, Founder of Conservative Party (Obituary)," *New York Times*, October 26, 1996.

32. Frank Lynn, "Charles E. Goodell, former senator, is dead at 60," *New York Times*, January 22, 1987.

33. "Gore Vidal," IMDb, accessed April 4, 2015, http://www.imdb.com/name/nm0000683/?ref_=fn_al_nm_1.

34. Tim Teeman, "For Gore Vidal, A Final Plot Twist, *New York Times*, November 8, 2013.

35. Ibid.

36. Tim Teeman, "For Gore Vidal, A Final Plot Twist, *New York Times*, November 8, 2013.

37. Debate Featuring William F. Buckley, Jr. and Gore Vidal. Democratic National Convention 1968, *ABC*, aired August 28, 1968, https://www.youtube.com/watch?v=ZY_nq4tfi24.

38. Lawrence Zuckerman, "How 'Firing Line' Transformed the Battleground," *New York Times*, December 18, 1999, accessed April 3, 2015, https://www.nytimes.com/books/00/07/16/specials/buckley-transformed.html.

39. Ibid.

40. Andrew Fergusen, "All Quiet on the Firing Line: William F. Buckley Jr. Flicks His Tongue and Skewers His Guests One Last Time," *CNN.com*, December 20, 1999, accessed April 3, 2015, http://www.cnn.com/ALLPOLITICS/time/1999/12/20/firing.line.html.

41. "William F. Buckley Biography," Essortment, January 1, 2011, accessed April 4, 2015, http://www.essortment.com/william-f-buckley-biography-20782.html.

42. Tsai, Michelle. "Why Did William F. Buckley Jr. Talk Like That?" *Slate*, February 28, 2008.

43. Roger Miller, Mike Stoller, and Jerry Lieber, "Kansas City Star" in *Greatest Hits* (Sony/ATV Tunes LLC, Jerry Leiber Music, Armo Music Corp., Sony/ATV Tree Publishing, Tree International, 1965). Accessed January 12, 2014, songlyrics.com. http://www.songlyrics.com/miller-roger/kansas-city-star-lyrics/.

44. "Cape Girardeau Flashback: Young Rush Lived At Home Once, Too," *Rush Limbaugh Online*, June 21, 2010.

45. Zev Chafets, *Rush Limbaugh: An Army of One*, New York: Sentinel Trade, 2011. 36, 38.

46. Ibid., 37,42.

47. John Derbyshire, "How Radio Wrecks the Right," *The American Conservative*, February 23, 2009, accessed March 3, 2015. http://www.theamericanconservative.com/articles/how-radio-wrecks-the-right/.

48. "Radio Group Buys Stations," *Omaha World Herald*, November 1, 1968.

49. "Starr announced plans for $4 million stock sale," *Broadcasting*, December 9, 1968, 55.

50. "FCC approves group purchases," *Broadcasting*, May 26, 1969, 46.

51. "WLOK – History," WLOK.com, accessed April 1, 2015, http://www.wlok.com/page.php?page_id=81.

52. Ibid.

53. "Another attempt to trade WCAM (AM)," *Broadcasting*, November 30, 1970, 22.

54. Ibid.

55. "President's Letter," *Annual Report* (Arlington House, Starr Broadcasting Group, 1970), 6.

56. Gordon McLendon, *Editorial*, Radio, KABL AM/FM, San Francisco, California, May 23, 1972.

57. *Ratings for San Francisco bay area*, Pulse Radio, Oct-Nov 1972.

58. Ronald Garay, *Gordon McLendon: The Maverick of Radio* (Westport, Connecticut: Greenwood Publishing Group,1992), 124-127.

59. "Activists make mark on Bay Area sale," *Broadcasting*, April, 24, 1972, 24.

60. Ibid.

61. "CCMC, KABL Establish Community Agreement." Creators Syndicate, April 24, 1972.

62. Ibid.

63. WNCN New York, Larry Miller, *WNCN aircheck/ flip to WQIV*, Radio, New York Radio Archive, November 7, 1974, accessed April 4, 2014, http://www.nyradioarchive.com/audio/WQIV_19741107_RF_Pt1.mp3.

64. Ibid.

65. Mildred Hall, "Radio Execs Await Format Rule," *Billboard*, November 2, 1974, accessed December 11, 2014, http://www.american radiohistory.com/Archive-Billboard/70s/1974/Billboard%201974-11-02.pdf.

66. Bill Buckley, "Buckley (Politely) Returns the Hand Grenade (Op-Ed article)," *New York*, October 7, 1974, 54.

67. Ibid., 56.

68. "Court OKs Format Switch...But," Mildred Hall, *Billboard*, November 9, 1974, accessed December 11, 2014, http://www.american radiohistory.com/Archive-Billboard/70s/1974/Billboard%201974-11-09.pdf.

69. "WNCN Comes Bach As Classical Station," *New York Times*, August 26, 1975, accessed November 29, 2014, http://www.nyradio archive.com/wqivfm.html.

70. Wallace White, "Allegro Vivace," Talk of the Town, *New Yorker*, September 8, 1975, 26.

71. "FCC v. WNCN Listeners Guild, 450 U.S. 582 (1981)," accessed February 28, 2015, https://supreme.justia.com/cases/federal/us/450/582/.

72. Ibid., Pp. 450 U. S. 593-604.

73. Ibid., P 450 U. S. 583.

74. Ibid., Pp 450 U.S.595-596.

75. Ibid.

76. William F. Buckley, Jr., *Airborne: A Sentimental Journey* (New York: Macmillan, 1976), 3.

77. Ibid., 6.

78. Ibid., 10.

79. Ibid., 82, 83.

80. Peter Beer, "Solomon V. Buckley," United States District Court, New Orleans Division, April 22, 1980, accessed November 9, 2014, https://casetext.com/case/solomon-v-buckley.

81. Securities and Exchange Commission Complaint against Starr Broadcasting, February 7, 1979.

82. Williams and Connolly, memo to the Securities and Exchange Commission, December 15, 2008. The senders of the memo were Buckley's personal attorneys.

83. Ibid., 9.

84. Ibid., 10.

85. Securities and Exchange Commission Complaint against Starr Broadcasting, February 7, 1979.

86. Securities and Exchange Commission Complaint against Starr Broadcasting, February 7, 1979.

87. Robert Johnson, "Inside Interview #37," interview by Jerry Del Colliano, *Inside Radio, Inc.*, 1977.

88. June Kronholz, "On the Firing Line: How William F. Buckley Got Starr Broadcasting to Bail Out His Firm," *Wall Street Journal*, October 24, 1978. This article appeared on the front page of the day's edition.

89. Williams and Connolly, memo to the Securities and Exchange Commission, December 15, 2008.

90. "SEC Says William F. Buckley Broke Law To Avoid Bankruptcy for Self and Others," *Wall Street Journal*, February 8, 1979.

91. Securities and Exchange Commission Complaint against Starr Broadcasting, February 7, 1979.

92. William F. Buckley, "Background Statement (press release)," February 7, 1979.

93. "Starr Principals in Mood to Sell," *Broadcasting*, January 16, 1978, 46.

94. Jerry Del Colliano "Suddenly Starr Broadcasting Is in Demand," *Inside Radio, Inc.*, March 13, 1978.

95. Jerry Del Colliano "Disney Agrees to Acquire Starr," *Inside Radio, Inc.*, May 15, 1978.

96. "FCC clears biggest deal ever," *Broadcasting*, June 11, 1979, 19-20.

97. Office of the White House Press Secretary, "Michael F. Starr Nomination (press release)," September 21, 1976.

98. Ben Gelman, "No stops is relief for SIU-C teacher," *Southern Illinoisan*, August 28, 1988, 39.

99. Dennis Rayburn, "Trekkie Vs.Trekker: The Great Debate," April 7, 2009, accessed March 20, 2015, https://www.roddenberry.com/index.php/communityblogs/index/detail/id/168.

100. Jacqueline Kennedy, "For President Kennedy, an Epilogue," interview by Theodore H. White, *Life*, 1963.

101. George W. Rutler, "Father Rutler on William F. Buckley Jr.," *Inside Catholic*, April 23, 2008, accessed January 29, 2015, http://www.catholic.org/clife/lent/story.php?id=27680.

102. "My Smoking Confessional," William F. Buckley, Jr., Universal Press Syndicate, December 3, 2007.

103. Christopher Buckley, *Losing Mum and Pup: A Memoir* (New York: Twelve Hachette Book Group Buckley, 2009), 146.

104. Christopher Buckley, *Losing Mum and Pup: A Memoir* (New York: Twelve Hachette Book Group Buckley, 2009), 210-215.

105. Howard Kurtz, "Christopher Buckley on His Book 'Losing Mum and Pup' (Book Review)," *Washington Post*, April 26, 2009, http://www.washingtonpost.com/wp-dyn/content/article/2009/04/23/ AR2009042304739.html.

106. Ibid.

107. Tom McGeveran, "Sam Tanenhaus to leave '*New York Times*' Book Review, become 'writer at large' for the paper," capitalnewyork.com, April 9, 2013, accessed April 3, 2015, http://www.capitalnewyork.com/ article/media/2013/04/8528922/sam-tanenhaus-leave-new-york-times-book-review-become-writer-large-pap.

108. Douglas E. Hall, *The Bergen News*, February 2008. Used by permission of the author.

109. Ibid.

Made in the USA
Coppell, TX
09 July 2021

58719632R20105